Who Is This Jesus Christ?

A prophet, a guru, one of the gods or more!

John S. Benjamin

WestBow
PRESS
A DIVISION OF THOMAS NELSON

ISBN: 978-1-4497-7076-1 (sc)
ISBN: 978-1-4497-7077-8 (e)
ISBN: 978-1-4497-7075-4 (hc)

Library of Congress Control Number: 2012918780

WestBow Press books may be ordered through booksellers or by contacting:

WestBow Press
A Division of Thomas Nelson
1663 Liberty Drive
Bloomington, IN 47403
www.westbowpress.com
1-(866) 928-1240

Unless otherwise noted, all scriptures references are taken from the New King James Version.

Printed in the United States of America

WestBow Press rev. date: 10/29/2012

Written to glorify and honor Jesus Christ

and

for the benefit of many, including my wife,
Marilyn; children, Sarah, Sabrina, and Sean;
and grandchildren, Anisha and Rashaun

Jesus said,

"And behold, I am coming quickly, and My reward is with Me, to give to every one according to his work. I am the Alpha and the Omega, the Beginning and the End, the First and the last." (Revelation 22: 12-13)

"I am the resurrection and the life. He who believes in Me, though he may die, he shall live. And whoever lives and believes in Me shall never die." (John 11: 25-26)

Table of Contents

Acknowledgement

My thanks to our son, Sean Jonathan, for his input and help in the completion of this book.

Introduction

All over the world, followers of almost every major religion venerate Christ in one form or another. Some acknowledge Him as a prophet, a guru, a teacher, a wise leader, a god, an advisor, or a guide. Others simply consider Him to have been a good person. Those who follow Him consider Him the Messiah, the King, the Priest, the Prophet, the Son of God, and more.

His birth, His life, and His works were all contrary to the laws of nature. His teachings are revolutionary and were relevant not only in His days but also today. He boggled the minds of the religious leaders as well as the rulers of the day. What He uttered was astounding to everyone. Has He changed the course of history for good? Was He a mere man, a mere prophet—or was He the image of God sent to fulfill a specific purpose or mission? In this book, I have attempted to shed some light on the life and mission of Jesus Christ.

The political, national, personal, behavioral, environmental, moral, ethical, and climatic landscape of this world is changing rapidly right before our eyes. We certainly live in turbulent times. The whole world seems to be in a total chaos and is groaning in pain. Amid all these uncertainties Humans are afraid of present and future, and not only are longing for inner peace,, but are seeking answers to these phenomena. When we see these events unfolding before our eyes, we ask ourselves a question: Is there a solution to these problems? Does the human race have answers to the calamities and problems we face? Will today's problems and challenges decrease and will things get better, or will they get worse?

Despite making giant strides in science and technology, we have not been successful in reducing human problems, let alone in eradicating them altogether. Science and psychology give us knowledge but cannot help us in any way to reach God. Humans are searching for answers that will reveal who we are, why we are here, and where we are going. We are looking for solutions to these problems. Amid all this chaos, confusion, and uncertainty, we wonder if God really cares. We seek to find out what the future holds for us. This book is for the benefit of those who are searching for answers to these questions and also for those searching for the truth. We will discover in this book what Jesus has said concerning all this and more.

Why are all these events happening? They are the results of sin that has entered this earth. Sin has severed the relationship between God and humankind. We chose our own path. Because of our disobedience, God could have annihilated humankind, but God, out of compassion promised to send the Messiah, who would save humankind from sin and guide and direct our path. God did this because He loves us and did not want us to perish. He is a loving and merciful God. It was imperative for Jesus to come into this world to restore the broken relation between God and man. There was no other way to restore this broken relationship. Only Jesus would qualify to do this, because of His heavenly origin and His sinless life. He did this by giving His sinless life as a ransom for our sin. Jesus Christ has given us the roadmap to eternal life.

While Jesus was on this earth, He forewarned His followers about the current events and the future of the world and pointed out that these events would take place in the end times. In this book, we will discuss these and some other events that have engulfed this world. We will dig into the Word of God, the Holy Bible, seek answers to many questions, and find out who Jesus Christ is.

Jesus has been the subject of controversy over the centuries. Nevertheless, He has affected and shaped the world in a very positive way. In the ensuing chapters of this book, I have attempted to touch very briefly on the life, mission, and person of Jesus Christ. The subject is vast, and volumes have been written and are still being written on it. This book will reveal and highlight a few aspects of His life and mission to whet your appetite, stimulate your thinking process, and challenge you to dig further and explore to find out more about Jesus Christ so you can draw your own conclusion about Him.

The purpose of this book is to introduce and share Jesus Christ with as many readers as possible, regardless of their religious affiliations and backgrounds, because Christ came for all of humanity. No one religion can claim exclusivity to the person of Jesus Christ. By knowing Him personally, one can find peace and joy amid all this turmoil, adversity, and unrest. We cannot find peace and joy in any other way.

We live in an age of information and communication. I urge you to read this book with an open mind, to reflect and ponder, and then either to dismiss it as fiction or to go deeper and seek the truth further. Jesus said, "And you shall know the truth, and the truth shall make you free. Therefore if the Son makes you free, you shall be free indeed" (John 8:32, 36).

Two prisoners looked out the cell window. One saw the stars and the other, sand.

It is my prayer that you find true peace and joy during your journey on earth and that you have the assurance that you will spend eternity with the One who created you. May God bless you.

Chapter 1

The Condition of This World

Let us just for a moment take a look around us. What do we see on the world scene? On the one hand, there is chaos, murders, wars, rumors of wars, sexual immorality, unfair business practices, family breakdown, misery, poverty, sickness, and more. On the other hand, climatic changes are taking place with an intensity and frequency never seen before. The human heart is failing because of fear; fear of the future, fear of uncertainty, fear of life—and the list goes on.

Despite astronomical advances in science and technology, we have failed to alleviate or minimize the problems humans are facing. If anything, human problems are on the increase, which adds to fears, worries, and anxieties. There is restlessness all around the world in almost every country. Ever since this world came into existence, we have seen very little peace, to say the least. Why all this? It is the result of sin that abounds all around us.

God created humans in His image and after His likeness. The Word of God says,

> Then God said, let Us make man in our image, according to Our likeness; let them have dominion over the fish of

the sea, over the birds of the air, and over the cattle over all the earth and over every creeping thing that creeps on the earth. So God created man in His own image; in the image of God He created him; male and female he created them. Then God blessed them and God said to them, "Be fruitful and multiply; fill the earth and subdue it; have dominion over the fish of the sea, over the birds of the air, and over every living thing that moves on the earth." And God said, "See I have given you every herb that yields seed which is on the face of all the earth, and every tree whose fruit yields seed; to you it shall be for food.

Then the Lord God took the man and put him in the garden of Eden to tend and keep it. And the Lord God commanded the man saying, "Of every tree of the garden you may freely eat; but of the tree of knowledge of good and evil you shall not eat, for in the day that you eat of it you shall surely die." (Genesis 1:26–29; 2:15–17)

According to God's command, Adam was to fill or populate and subdue the earth, exercise dominion over all the animals, take care of the garden of Eden, and eat its fruit. God also commanded Adam not to eat the fruit of the Tree of the Knowledge of Good and Evil.

Adam disobeyed God and ate the forbidden fruit, which resulted in sin and separation from God. God is a holy God, and He cannot see sin. The relationship between all-holy God and sinful man was thus broken, resulting in separation between God and humankind. This separation would be passed on to us all.

Light and darkness cannot coexist. Therefore, this act of disobedience not only brought separation but also spiritual and physical death to Adam and humanity. Spiritual death occurred the moment Adam disobeyed God's command, while physical death started from that moment and would take place in the future. God created us to live forever in His presence. He did not create us to die, but because Adam acted against the will and command of God and disobeyed Him, death entered into humanity. Every person who is born will have to die one day. Therefore, it is said that humans are mortal.

Let's read the account of human disobedience to God's command as written in the Bible.

> Now the serpent was more cunning than any beast of the field which the Lord God had made. And he said to the woman (Eve), "Has God indeed said, 'You shall not eat of every tree of the garden'?" And the woman (Eve) said to the serpent, "We may eat the fruit of the trees of the garden; but of the fruit of the tree which is in the midst of the garden, God has said, 'You shall not eat of it, nor shall you touch it, lest you die.'" And the serpent said to the woman, "You will not surely die. For God knows that in the day you eat of it your eyes will be opened, and you will be like God, knowing good and evil." So when the woman saw that the tree was good for food, that it was pleasant to the eyes, and a tree desirable to make one wise, she took of its fruit and ate. She also gave to her husband with her, and he ate. Then the eyes of both of them were opened, and they knew that they were naked; and they sewed fig leaves together and made themselves coverings. And they heard the sound of the Lord God walking in the garden in the cool of the day, and Adam and his wife hid themselves from the presence of the Lord God among the trees of the garden. Then the

Lord God called to Adam and said to him, "Where are you?" So he said, "I heard Your voice in the garden, and I was afraid because I was naked; and I hid myself." And He said, "Who told you that you were naked? Have you eaten from the tree of which I commanded you that you should not eat?" Then the man said, "The woman whom you gave to be with me, she gave me of the tree, and I ate." And the Lord God said to the woman, "What is this you have done?" And the woman said, "The serpent deceived me, and I ate." (Genesis 3:1–13)

What we see here is Satan putting doubt in Eve's mind; she believed him and disbelieved God. She disbelieved the One who created her and instead believed the lie and deception of Satan and rejected God's command. Why? Because she entered into a dialogue with Satan, and as a result he deceived her. This would not have happened if she had taken authority over Satan and rejected his talk.

God had given Adam and Even dominion over everything. How many times we sin against our Creator and believe the lie of Satan! If we entertain any thought that is contrary to God's command, we commit a sin. We are not to open up a dialogue with Satan. If we do, we make ourselves vulnerable. We are to reject right away any thought that is contrary to God's command. When Eve and her husband, Adam, disobeyed God and ate the forbidden fruit, their eyes were opened, and they realized they were naked. And they tried to cover their nakedness with fig leaves.

Adam and Eve heard the sound of the Lord God walking in the garden in the cool of the day, and they hid themselves from the presence of the Lord God among the trees. Yet we cannot hide or cover our nakedness from God. We are just not capable of doing this, because God knows everything about us. Satan is cunning and a deceiver. He is deceiving millions upon millions of people all over the world.

God asked Adam if he ate the forbidden fruit, and instead of acknowledging his sin, Adam put the blame on the woman. Eve in turn blamed the serpent. When at fault, we try to shift the blame onto someone other than ourselves. Any time Satan tempts anyone, he does not reveal the consequences of sin. Satan didn't tell Adam and Eve that the day they ate of the forbidden fruit they would face not only separation from God but also spiritual and physical death—eternal damnation.

Promise of the Messiah

So the Lord God said to the serpent: "Because you have done this, you are cursed more than all cattle, and more than every beast of the field; on your belly you shall go, and you shall eat dust all the days of your life. And I will put enmity between you and the woman, and between your seed and her seed; He shall bruise your head and you shall bruise His heel." To the woman He said: "I will greatly multiply your sorrow and your conception; in pain you shall bring forth children; your desire shall be for your husband, and he shall rule over you." Then to Adam He said, "Because you have heeded the voice of your wife, and have eaten from the tree of which I commanded you, saying, 'you shall not eat of it': "Cursed is the ground for your sake; in toil you shall eat of it all the days of your life. Both thorns and thistles it shall bring forth for you, and you shall eat the herb of the field. In the sweat of your face you shall eat bread till you return to the ground, for out of it you were taken; for dust you are and to dust you shall return." (Genesis 3:14–19)

We see the consequence of sin here. God deals with the serpent, with Adam, and with Eve.

The serpent personifies Satan. God tells the serpent, 'I will put enmity between you and the *woman*, and between your seed and *her Seed*; He shall bruise your head and you shall bruise His heel' (emphasis added). God did not say, "I will put enmity between you and the seed of *man* or seed of Adam." He said, "I will put enmity between you and the *woman*" (emphasis added). Why "Seed of *woman*" and not seed of *man*? God is pointing to Jesus' *sinless* birth. In the natural, humans are born as a result of union between a man and a woman, but Jesus' birth was not the result of such a union. He was born of the Virgin Mary through the Holy Ghost. He was born contrary to the law of nature.

Right here God is promising the Messiah who would come to this earth and give His life as a living and pure sacrifice for the sins of humanity. No human could have done that, because of sin that entered into our race through disobedience. It had to be a pure and unblemished sacrifice that no human could have given, because every human inherited sin from Adam. Jesus was born sinless and lived a sinless life.

Jesus' Sinless Birth

Let's read the account of Jesus' birth, which throws further light on the fact that it was sinless.

> Now in the sixth month the angel Gabriel was sent by God to a city of Galilee named Nazareth, to a virgin betrothed to a man whose name was Joseph, of the house of David. The virgin's name was Mary. And having come in, the angel said to her, "Rejoice, highly favored one, the Lord is with you;

blessed are you among women!" But when she saw him, she was troubled at his saying, and considered what manner of greeting this was. Then the angel said to her, "Do not be afraid, Mary, for you have found favor with God. And behold you will conceive in your womb and bring forth a Son, and shall call His name Jesus. He will be great, and will be called the Son of the Highest; and the Lord God will give Him the throne of His father David. And He will reign over the house of Jacob forever, and of His kingdom there will be no end." Then Mary said to the angel, "How can this be, since I do not know a man?" And the angel answered and said to her, *"The Holy Spirit will come upon you and the power of the highest will over shadow you; therefore, also that Holy One who is to be born will be called the Son of God."* (Luke 1:26–35, emphasis added)

The Purpose of Jesus' Birth

"He shall bruise your head and you shall bruise His heel." Here God is talking about His Son Jesus Christ: He would bruise Satan's head, and Satan would bruise His heel. Jesus would come and crush Satan's head. Satan did bruise Jesus' heel by crucifying Him, but Jesus rose victoriously from the dead on the third day, thereby crushing Satan's head once and for all. Sin was the reason for Christ's coming into this world and the cause for which He endured the cross. This was the purpose for which He came to this earth.

We saw earlier that after Adam and Eve sinned, they tried to cover themselves with fig leaves. Humans are totally helpless and incapable of covering or getting rid of their sins. Only God can cover sins. Genesis 3:21 says, "For Adam and his wife the Lord

God made tunics of skin, and clothed them." God slaughtered an *innocent* animal to make tunics to cover them. This act of God is the reflection of the ultimate sinless sacrifice Jesus would make in the future. Because Jesus was innocent and without sin, only He could give His life for the sin of mankind.

Sin came into this world through one man, Adam, which he passed on to the future generations. No amount of animal sacrifices could wipe out or eradicate sin. We cannot cover our sins by our own efforts and in our own strength. Just as a baby snake gets its venom from father and mother snake, we get our sinful nature from Adam and Eve. All humankind has inherited Adam's DNA. Therefore, we are sinners by nature; sin is in our nature. Only a sinless sacrifice could eradicate sin. There was no other way. Therefore, God sent His Son Jesus Christ, who was not only born sinless but also lived a sinless life. Jesus would ultimately give His life as ransom for the sins of humankind, and by doing so save us from eternal damnation, give us life eternal, and restore the broken relation between God and us.

God hates sin but loves us: "For God so loved the world that He gave His only begotten Son, that whoever believes in Him should not perish but have everlasting life" (John 3:16). God could not see anyone damned eternally. There was only one way to save us from death: a pure, sinless, and unblemished sacrificed had to be made. God is merciful and loving; therefore He sent His only begotten Son Jesus Christ to save all humankind from eternal damnation. Jesus' sacrifice on the cross set humankind free from the bondage of sin. "Whoever commits sin also commits lawlessness, and sin is lawlessness. And you know that He [Christ] was manifested to take away our sins, and in Him there is no sin" (1 John 3:4–5).

This was the reason Jesus came on this earth: He gave His

life to free us all from sin and eternal damnation. Our sin was the reason Jesus came into this world. He paid the highest imaginable price by shedding His own blood so reconciliation between God and humankind could be possible.

Jesus said,

- "I did not come to call the righteous, but sinners, to repentance" (Matthew 9:13).
- "For the Son of Man has come to save that which was lost" (Matthew 18:11).
- "Those who are well have no need of a physician, but those who are sick. I did not come to call the righteous, but sinners, to repentance" (Mark 2:17).
- "For even the Son of Man did not come to be served, but to serve, and to give His life a ransom for many" (Mark 10:45).
- "For the Son of Man did not come to destroy men's lives but to save them" (Luke 9:56).
- "For God did not send His Son into the world to condemn the world, but that the world through Him might be saved" (John 3:17).
- "And this is the will of Him who sent Me, that everyone who sees the Son and believes in Him may have everlasting life; and I will raise him up at the last day" (John 6:40).
- "I am the living bread which came down from heaven. If anyone eats of this bread, he will live forever; and the bread that I shall give is My flesh, which I shall give for the life of the world" (John 6:51).
- "I have come as a light into the world, that whoever believes in Me should not abide in darkness. And if anyone hears My words and does not believe, I do not judge him; for I did

not come to judge the world but to save the world" (John 12:46–47).

- "For this cause I was born, and for this cause I have come into the world, that I should bear witness to the truth. Everyone who is of the truth hears My voice" (John 18:37).

Chapter 2

The Birth of Jesus Christ

The following is the account of Jesus' birth as recorded in the Bible:

> Now in the sixth month the angel Gabriel was sent by God to a city of Galilee named Nazareth, to a virgin betrothed to a man whose name was Joseph, of the house of David. The virgin's name was Mary. And having come in, the angel said to her, "Rejoice, highly favored one, the Lord is with you; blessed are you among women!" But when she saw him, she was troubled at his saying, and considered what manner of greeting this was. Then the angel said to her, "Do not be afraid, Mary, for you have found favor with God. And behold, you will conceive in your womb and bring forth a Son, and shall call His name Jesus. He will be great, and will be called the Son of the Highest; and the Lord God will give him the throne of His father David. And He will reign over the house of Jacob forever, and of His kingdom there will be no end." Then Mary said to the angel, "How can this be, since I do not know a

man?" And the angel answered and said to her, "The Holy Spirit will come upon you, and the power of the Highest will overshadow you; therefore, also the Holy One who is to be born will be called the Son of God. Now indeed, Elizabeth your relative has also conceived a son in her old age; and this is now the sixth month for her who was called barren. For with God nothing will be impossible." Then Mary said, "Behold the maiservant of the Lord! Let it be to me according to your word." And the angel departed from her. Luke 1:26-38

Christ Is Born

And it came to pass in those days that a decree went out from Caesar Augustus that all the world should be registered. This census first took place while Quirinius was governing Syria. So all went to be registered, everyone to his own city. And Joseph also went up from Galilee, out of the city of Nazareth, into Judea, to the city of David, which is called Bethlehem, because he was of the house and lineage of David, to be registered with Mary, his betrothed wife, who was with child. So it was, that while they were there, the days were completed for her to be delivered. And she brought forth her firstborn Son and wrapped Him in swaddling cloths, and laid Him in a manger, because there was no room for them in the inn. Luke 2: 1-7

The Angels Announce Jesus to the Shepherds

Now there were in the same country shepherds living out in the fields, keeping watch over their flock by night. And behold, an angel of the Lord stood before them, and the glory of the Lord shone around them, and they were greatly afraid. Then the angel said to them, "Do not be afraid, for behold, I bring you good tidings of great joy which will be to all people. For there is born to you this day in the city of David a Savior who is Christ the Lord. And this will be the sign to you: You will find a babe wrapped in swaddling cloths, lying in a manger." And suddenly there was with the angels a multitude of the heavenly hosts praising God and saying; "Glory to God in the highest, And on earth peace, good will toward men." (Luke 2:8-14)

What an amazing story of the birth of Jesus Christ! Angel Gabriel told Mary:

a. "And behold, you will conceive in your womb and bring forth a Son, and shall call His name Jesus." Luke 1: 31
b. "And the angel answered and said to her (Mary), The Holy Spirit will come upon you, and the power of the Highest will overshadow you; therefore, also that Holy One who is to be born will be called the Son of God." Luke 1: 35

The above verses clearly state that Jesus Christ, was:
a. Born in human flesh, and
b. (b) He is the Son of God.

Seven hundred years before the birth of Christ, the prophet Isaiah prophesied about Christ: "For unto us a Child is born, unto us a Son is given; and the government will be upon His shoulder. And His name will be called Wonderful, Counselor, Mighty God, Everlasting Father, Prince of Peace" (Isaiah 9:6).

"Unto us a Child is born" signifies Christ taking human form. "Unto us a Son is given" signifies God is sending His Son Jesus Christ to this earth; it also signifies Jesus' heavenly origin.

Isaiah goes further and prophesies about Jesus Christ: "Therefore the Lord Himself will give you a sign: Behold, the virgin shall conceive and bear a Son and shall call His name Immanuel." Isaiah 7:14

Matthew writes about Jesus, "And she (Mary) will bring forth a Son, and you shall call His name Jesus, for He will save His people from their sins" (Matthew 1:21).

The existence of the Son of God did not commence with His birth in Bethlehem. He is spoken of as the Son before He became a man. Another prophet of God, Micah, prophesied about Christ: "But you, Bethlehem Ephrathah, though you are little among the thousands of Judah, Yet out of you shall come forth to Me The One to be ruler in Israel, Whose goings forth have been from of old, From everlasting." Micah 5:2.

John the evangelist also mentioned the pre-existence of Christ in his gospel: "In the beginning was the Word, and the Word was with God, and the Word was God. He was in the beginning with God. All things were made through Him, and without Him nothing was made that was made" (John 1:1–3).

Centuries before Jesus Christ took human form, He appeared to God's people from time to time as an "Angel of the Lord" and is identified as God. For example, Jesus appeared to Moses as the Angel of the Lord:

> Now Moses kept the flock of Jethro his father-in-law, the priest of Midian. And he led the flock to the back of the desert, and came to Horeb, the mountain of God. And the Angel of the Lord appeared to him in a flame of fire from

the midst of a bush. So he looked, and behold, the bush burned with fire, but the bush was not consumed. Then Moses said, "I will now turn aside and see this great sight, why the bush does not burn." So when the Lord saw that he turned aside to look, God called to him from the midst of the bush and said, "Moses, Moses!" And he said, "Here I am." Then He said, "Do not draw near this place. Take your sandals off your feet, for the place where you stand is holy ground." Moreover He said, I am the God of your father—the God of Abraham, the God of Isaac, and the God of Jacob." And Moses hid his face for he was afraid to look upon God. (Exodus 3:1–6)

While Christ was fully man, He was also fully God, as these facts indicate:

- He was is called God: "In the beginning was the Word, and the Word was with God and the Word was God" (John 1:1).
- Being God, Jesus has the power to forgive sins as only God can do: "But that you may know that the Son of Man has power on earth to forgive sins" (Mark 2:10).
- He has the power to create: "For by Him all things were created that are in heaven and that are on earth, visible and invisible, whether thrones or dominions or principalities or powers. All things were created through Him and for Him" (Colossians 1:16).
- He has attributes that only God could have, such as truth: "Jesus said to Him, 'I am the way, the truth and the life. No one comes to the Father except through me. If you had known Me, you would have known My Father also; and

from now on you know Him and have seen Him'" (John 14:6-7).

- Jesus is omniscient (is all knowing): "Now when He was in Jerusalem at the Passover, during the feast, many believed in His name when they saw the signs which He did. But Jesus did not commit Himself to them, because He knew all men, and had no need that anyone should testify of man, for He knew what was in man" (John 2:23–25).

- He claimed equality with God: "I and My Father are one" (John 10:30).

- He claimed to be eternal: "Your father Abraham rejoiced to see My day, and he saw and was glad—Most assuredly I say to you, before Abraham was, I AM" (John 8:56–58).

- He was worshipped: "And behold, a leper came and worshipped Him, saying, 'Lord, if You are willing, You can make me clean.' Then Jesus put out His hand and touched him, saying, 'I am willing; be cleansed.' And immediately his leprosy was cleansed" Matthew. 8:2–3). Also, "And He [Jesus] led them out as far as Bethany, and He lifted up His hands and blessed them. Now it came to pass, while He blessed them, that He was parted from them and carried up into heaven. And they worshipped Him, and returned to Jerusalem with great joy" (Luke 24:50–52). And "Jesus heard that they had cast him out; and when He had found him, He said to him, do you believe in the Son of God?" He answered and said, 'Who is He, Lord, that I may believe in Him?' And Jesus said to him, 'You have both seen Him and it is He who is talking with you.' Then he said, 'Lord, I believe' and he worshipped Him' (John 9:35–38).

Jesus Son of God

What do we mean when we say Jesus is the Son of God? Does it mean that Jesus is the Son of God in the sense of a human father and a son? God did not get married and have a son. Jesus is God's Son in that He was conceived in Mary by the Holy Spirit: "The angel answered and said to her, 'The Holy Spirit will come upon you, and the power of the Most High will overshadow you; therefore, also, that Holy One who is to be born will be called the Son of God'" (Luke 1:35).

Jesus is God's Son in the sense that He is God made manifest in human form, according to John the evangelist, "And the Word became flesh and dwelt among us, and we beheld His glory, the glory as of the only begotten of the Father, full of grace and truth." (John 1:1, 14).

Jesus Himself said that He is the Son of God. When the high priest asked Jesus if He was the Son of God, He answered, "It is as you said. Nevertheless I say to you, hereafter you will see the Son of Man sitting at the right hand of the Power, and coming on the clouds of heaven." Matthew 26: 64. Nowhere in the Bible it is said that God has a wife and through procreation a son, whose name is Jesus.

Jesus is also called the Son of God because He was faithful and obedient to God. He is the Son of God in the sense that His resemblance, characteristics, and qualities are in likeness of God.

Chapter 3

Purpose of His First Coming

He Came to Save

"And she will bring for a Son, and you shall call His name Jesus, for He will save His people from their sins." (Matthew 1:21)

Then Jesus entered and passed through Jericho. Now behold, there was a man named Zacchaeus who was a chief tax collector, and he was rich. And he sought to see who Jesus was, but could not because of the crowd, for he was of short stature. So he ran ahead and climbed up into a sycamore tree to see Him, for He was going to pass that way. And when Jesus came to the place, He looked up and saw him, and said to him, "Zacchaeus, make haste and come down, for today, I must stay at your house." So he made haste and came down, and received Him joyfully. But when they saw it, they all murmured, saying, "He has gone to be a guest with a man who is a sinner." Then Zacchaeus stood and said to the Lord, "Look, Lord, I give half of my goods to the poor; and if I have taken anything from anyone by false accusation, I restore four-fold." And Jesus said to him, "Today salvation has come to this house, because he also is a son of Abraham; for the Son of Man has come to seek and to save that which was lost." (Luke 19:1–10)

[Jesus said,] "For the Son of Man has come to save that which was lost. What do you think? If a man has a hundred sheep, and one of them goes astray, does he not leave the ninety-nine and go to the mountains to seek the one that is straying. And if he should find it, assuredly, I say to you, he rejoices more over that sheep than over the ninety-nine that did not go astray. Even so it is not the will of your Father who is in heaven that one of these little ones should perish." (Matthew 18:11–14)

Then all the tax collectors and sinners drew near to Him to hear Him. And the Pharisees and scribes murmured, saying, "This man receives sinners and eats with them." So He spoke this parable to them, saying: "What man of you, having a hundred sheep, if he loses one of them, does not leave the ninety-nine in the wilderness, and go after the one which is lost until he finds it? And when he has found it, he lays it on his shoulders, rejoicing. And when he comes home, he calls together his friends and neighbors, saying to them, 'Rejoice with me, for I have found my sheep which was lost!' I say to you that likewise there will be more joy in heaven over one sinner who repents than over ninety-nine just persons who need no repentance." (Luke 15:1–7)

We have heard that "Christ died to save sinners." Again, humans by birth and by nature are sinners. Christ came to take the penalty for sin on Himself and to die in place of sinners. He knew the purpose and reason of His coming to this earth, which was to save humankind from sin and eternal damnation and to restore the relationship between humans and God. Being the Son of God and completely sinless, only He could qualify to save humankind. He did this by laying down His life willingly as a ransom for sinful humankind, and as such, his death on the cross was a propitiatory sacrifice.

Before dying on the cross Jesus said, "It is finished," meaning the redemptive work He came to do was completed. Sinful humankind desperately needed this supernatural Jesus, because only this supernatural Jesus could bridge the gap between us and the all-holy God. Though for this cause He died an excruciating, painful, and humiliating death on the cross, in retrospect His followers realized that this death was not in vain. They realized that truly Jesus was the Messiah. They also realized that the cross was not a tragedy, but a symbol of triumph over sin and death.

Thus Jesus Christ is indeed the Savior of this world, the Son of God and the Messiah. His death on the cross was not the conclusion of His ministry on this earth; His resurrection marks the triumph over sin and death. He conquered death by His resurrection and ascended into heaven from where He is coming again on this earth to rule with truth and justice. There will be peace on this earth under His rule.

He Came to Serve

Jesus is the King, the Messiah, the Creator and Lord of the universe. He deserves to be adored, served, and worshipped. Instead,

He chose to serve the humanity and set an example of humility and service to better others' lives. Jesus told His disciples, "You know that those who are considered rulers over the Gentiles lord it over them, and their great ones exercise authority over them. Yet is shall not be so among you; but whoever desires to become great among you shall be your servant. And whoever of you desires to be first shall be slave of all. For even the Son of Man did not come to be served, but to serve, and to give His life a ransom for many" (Mark 10:42–45). He washed His disciples' feet to teach them and all His followers to be servants to others.

He Came to Change the World.

No man has changed and impacted the earth the way Jesus has. After all, He is the Creator of this earth.

> The Lord reigns, Let the earth rejoice; Let the multitudes of isles be glad! Clouds and darkness surround Him; Righteousness and justice are the foundation of His throne. A fire goes before Him, and burns up His enemies round about. His lightnings light the world; the earth sees and trembles. The mountains melt like wax at the presence of the Lord, at the presence of the Lord of the whole earth. The heavens declare His righteousness, and all the people see His glory. (Psalm 97:1–6)

He came to demonstrate love, justice, and truth. He said, " For this cause I was born, and for this cause I have come into the world, that I should bear witness to the truth. Everyone who is of the truth hears My voice" (John 18:37).

Jesus is God. His message is love. He was also fully human. He became tired, hungry, sad, and angry, just like any other human. While He was on this earth, He went to work as any other man. Being human, He was also tempted just like any other man: "but [He] was in all points tempted as we are, yet without sin. Let us therefore come boldly to the throne of grace, that we may obtain mercy and find grace to help in time of need." Hebrews 4:15-16. Being sinless, only He could qualify to bear sins of the world. John the Baptist said about Jesus, "Behold! The Lamb of God who takes away the sin of the world! This is He of whom I said, after me comes a Man who is preferred before me, for He was before me" (John 1:29–30).

Centuries before Jesus came to this earth, Isaiah prophesied about Jesus and wrote, "Therefore the Lord Himself will give you a sign: Behold, the virgin shall conceive and bear a Son, and shall call His name Immanuel." Isaiah 7: 14. Immanuel means "God with us." Jesus, the Son of God became man so that, as a sinless human, He could pay the price for the crimes of humanity. He took our sins on the cross, so we bear them no more. God is judge, and all humankind is guilty of sin and therefore the offender. Only the judge can name the penalty, which is payable by the offender. Therefore, to pay the penalty of sin on behalf of humanity, God had to become human Who was completely pure, unblemished, and without sin. Now that the penalty has been paid in full, the decision to accept Jesus as the Savior is up to each person.

He Came to Make the Holy Spirit Available

By nature, humans are weak and can give in to temptation. Jesus said, "What comes out of a man that defiles a man. For from within, out of the heart of men, proceed evil thoughts, adulteries, fornications, murders, thefts, covetousness, wickedness, deceit, licentiousness, an evil eye, blasphemy, pride, foolishness. All these evil things come from within and defile a man" (Mark 7:20–23).

Jesus, knowing the sinful nature of humans, told His disciples, "I am the vine, you are the branches. He who abides in Me, and I in him, bears much fruit; for without Me you can do nothing." John 15:5. He came to make the Holy Spirit available. He said, "But you shall receive power when the Holy Spirit has come upon you; and you shall be witnesses to Me in Jerusalem, and in all Judea and Samaria, and to the end of the earth"(Acts 1:8). He also said, " And I will pray the Father, and He will give you another Helper, that He may abide with you forever" (John 14:16). The Helper, or the Comforter, resides within the heart and mind of every regenerated or born again Christian. The Holy Spirit gives testimony of Jesus: "But when the Helper comes, whom I shall send to you from the Father, the Spirit of truth who proceeds from the Father, He will testify of Me" (John 15:26).

He Came to Bring the Gospel of the Kingdom of God

Gospel means "good news." Jesus preached the good news: "Jesus came to Galilee preaching the gospel of the kingdom of God, and saying, 'The time is fulfilled, and the kingdom of God is at hand. Repent, and believe in the gospel'" (Mark 1:14–15). While Jesus was preaching the kingdom of God, He also met the needs of people who followed Him. For example, He healed the sick:

> Now when the sun was setting, all those who had anyone sick with various diseases brought them to Him; and He laid His hands on every one of them and healed them. And demons also came out of many, crying out and saying, "You are the Christ, the Son of God! And He, rebuking them,

did not allow them to speak, for they knew that He was the Christ. Now when it was day, He departed and went into a deserted place. And the crowd sought Him and came to Him, and tried to keep Him from leaving them; but He said to them, "I must preach the kingdom of God to the other cities also, because for this purpose I have been sent." (Luke 4:40–43)

Now it came to pass, afterward, that He went through every city and village, preaching and bringing the glad tidings of the kingdom of God. And the twelve were with Him. (Luke 8:1)

"Then He called His twelve disciples together and gave them power and authority over all demons, and to cure diseases. He sent them to preach the kingdom of God and to heal the sick." (Luke 9:1–2)

He Came to Build His Church.

God loves the world. Therefore, He sent Jesus Christ to redeem the world. After Jesus finished the redemptive work, and before He ascended into heaven, He commanded His disciples to preach the gospel (good news) to the world, saying, "Go therefore and make disciples of all the nations, baptizing them in the name of the Father and of the Son and of the Holy Spirit, teaching them to observe all things that I have commanded you; and lo, I am with you always, even to the end of the age" (Matthew 28:19–20).

After Jesus sacrificed His life for the sins of humanity, He wanted the truth and the gospel of the kingdom of God made available to the world. Before He ascended to heaven, he prayed to the Father,

"Father, the hour has come. Glorify Your Son, that Your Son also may glorify You, as You have given Him authority over all flesh, that He should give eternal life to as many as You have given Him. And this is eternal life, that they may know You, the only true God, and Jesus Christ whom You have sent. I have glorified You on the earth. I have finished the work which You have given Me to do. And now, O Father, glorify Me together with Yourself, with the glory which I had with You before the world was." (John 17:1–5)

Jesus gave the truth to His disciples and wanted them to spread His truth further so others may also be benefited and saved. He said,

"This is my commandment, that you love one another as I have loved you. Greater love has no one than this, than to lay down one's life for his friends. You are My friends if you do whatever I command you. No longer do I call you servants, for a servant does not know what his master is doing; but I have called you friends, for all things that I heard from My Father I have made known to you. You did not choose Me, but I chose you and appointed you that you should go and bear fruit, and that your fruit should remain, that whatever you ask the Father in My name He may give you. These things I command you, that you love one another." (John 15:12–17)

Chapter 4

Jesus' Earthly Ministry

He Revolutionized the World

Jesus taught His disciples and the multitudes that followed Him to love God and love one another. He revolutionized the world through His teachings, which will be discussed in the following chapter.

Jesus met all human needs. He healed the sick and the brokenhearted, cleansed the lepers, raised the dead, fed the hungry, forgave sins, preached the gospel of the kingdom of God, prepared and equipped His disciples to carry out His mission, showed the way, revealed the truth—and the list goes on. He was merciful and compassionate toward the downtrodden, the outcasts, and the destitute.

Jesus Has All Authority

While Jesus was on this earth, He demonstrated His divine authority over people. His teachings were revolutionary, authoritative and contrary to the common belief of His day. On one occasion as He was addressing the multitude, He said,

> Not everyone who says to Me, Lord, Lord, shall enter the kingdom of heaven, but he who does the will of My Father in heaven. Many will say to Me in that Lord, Lord, have we not prophesied in Your name, cast out demons in Your name, and done many wonders in Your name? And then I will declare to them, I never knew you; depart from Me, you who practice lawlessness! Therefore whoever hears these sayings of Mine, and does them, I will liken him to a wise man who built his house on the rock: and the rain descended, the floods came, and the winds blew and beat on that house, and it did not fall, for it was founded on the rock. Now everyone who hears these sayings of Mine, and does not do them, will be like a foolish man who built his house on the sand, and the rain descended, the floods came, and the winds blew and beat on that house; and it fell. And great was its fall." And so it was, when Jesus had ended these sayings, that the people were astonished at His teaching, for He taught them as one having authority, and not as the scribes. (Matthew 7:21–29)

The foregoing passage clearly indicates that His teachings were authoritative because of the fact that His origin was heavenly. People were astonished at His teaching, for He taught them with authority.

> He also demonstrated His heavenly authority by forgiving sins. And again He entered Capernaum after some days, and it was heard that He was in the house. Immediately

many gathered together, so that there was no longer room to receive them, not even near the door. And He preached the word to them. Then they came to Him, bringing a paralytic who was carried by four men. And when they could not come near Him because of the crowd, they uncovered the roof where He was. And when they had broken through, they let down the bed on which the paralytic was lying. When Jesus saw their faith, He said to the paralytic, "Son your sins are forgiven you." But some of the scribes were sitting there and reasoning in their hearts, "Why does this man speak blasphemies like this? Who can forgive sins but God alone?" And immediately when Jesus perceived in His spirit that they reasoned thus within themselves, He said to them, "Why do you reason about these things in your hearts? Which is easier, to say to the paralytic, your sins are forgiven you, or to say, arise, take up your bed and walk? But that you may know that the Son of Man has power on earth to forgive sins." He said to the paralytic, "I say to you arise, take up your bed, and go your way to your house." (Mark 2:1–11)

Jesus Himself said, "All authority has been given to Me in heaven and on earth." (Matthew 28:18)

On judgment day, Jesus will sit in the judgment seat and will judge people from all nations and races.

Jesus Meets Spiritual, Emotional, and Physical Needs.

Jesus was a humanitarian. He was sensitive not only to people's spiritual and emotional needs, but also to their physical needs. Here's one instance:

When Jesus heard it, He departed from there by boat to a deserted place by Himself. But when the multitude heard it, they followed Him on foot from the cities. And when Jesus went out He saw a great multitude; and He was moved with compassion for them, and healed their sick. When it was evening, His disciples came to Him, saying, "This is a deserted place, and the hour is already late. Send the multitude away, that they may go into the villages and buy themselves food." But Jesus said to them," They do not need to go away. You give them something to eat." And they said to Him, "We have here only five loaves and two fish." He said, "Bring them here to Me." Then He commanded the multitudes to sit down on the grass. And He took the five loaves and the two fish, and looking up to heaven, He blessed and broke and gave to the multitudes. So they all ate and were filled, and they took up twelve baskets full of the fragments that remained. Now those who had eaten were about five thousand men, besides women and children. (Matthew 14:13–21)

He Came to Show God's Love

Christ showed God's love.

For God so loved the world that He gave His only begotten Son that whoever believes in Him should not perish but have everlasting life. For God did not send His Son into the world to condemn the world, but that the world through Him might be saved. He who believes in Him is not condemned; but he who does not believe is condemned already, because he has not believed in the name of the only begotten Son of God. (John 3:16–18)

To save us from sin, Jesus refused a crown and willingly accepted cruel death so we might have life. The grave could not keep Him. He rose again from the dead and ascended into heaven. His resurrection is the greatest event of His ministry. It is amazing to know that God loved us when we were still sinners; we were still under the death penalty when He called us. "But God demonstrates His own love toward us, in that while we were still sinners, Christ died for us" (Romans 5:8).

Jesus loves us so much that He wants to spend eternity with us. Nothing gives Him more joy than the fact that He will be together with those who believed in Him. "Looking unto Jesus, the author and finisher of our faith, who for the joy that was set before Him endured the cross, despising the shame, and has sat down at the right hand of the throne of God" (Hebrews 12:2). Jesus considers it a joy to be with His saints in heaven for eternity. For this joy, He endured the worst possible kind of physical punishment and bore the cross willingly so whoever believes in Him will not perish but have everlasting life. For this joy He underwent scourging and crucifixion, which was the most brutal and torturous form of execution. Isaiah prophesied, "Just as many were astonished at you, so His visage [appearance] was marred [defaced, disfigured] more than any man, and His form more than the sons of men" (Isaiah 52:14).

Jesus willingly took our curse and the death penalty on Himself. The sin Adam committed, passed on to us and as such the penalty of sin had to be paid. Jesus paid that penalty on the cross and by doing that He has redeemed us from the curse of the law, having become a curse for us (for it is written, 'cursed is everyone who hangs on a tree')" (Galatians 3:13).

No matter how sinful we are, when we genuinely repent and are baptized, God promises complete forgiveness. Only Christ's sacrifice can permanently cleanse and forgive us.

He Transformed the Lives of Outcasts and Sinners

Jesus touched and transformed lives of the outcasts and sinners who consequently changed the world for better.

> And as He passed by, He saw Levi the son of Alphaeus sitting at the tax office, and said to him, follow Me. And he arose and followed Him. Now it happened, as He was dining in Levi's house, that many tax collectors and sinners also sat together with Jesus and His disciples; for there were many, and they followed Him. And when the scribes and the Pharisees saw Him eating with the tax collectors and sinners, they said to His disciples, how is it that He eats and drinks with tax collectors and sinners. When Jesus heard it, He said to them, "Those who are well have no need of a physician, but those who are sick. I did not come to call the righteous, but sinners, to repentance." (Mark 2:14–17)

He Brought Peace to Human Hearts

Jesus brought peace to human hearts. Before ascending to heaven, He said these comforting words to His disciples,

> If anyone loves Me, he <u>will</u> keep My word; and My Father will love him, and We will come to him and make Our home with him. He who does not love Me does not keep My words; and the word which you hear is not Mine but the Father's who sent Me. These things I have spoken to you while being present with you. But the Helper, the Holy Spirit, whom the Father will send in My name, He will teach you all things, and bring to your remembrance all

things that I said to you. Peace I leave with you, My peace I give to you; not as the world gives do I give to you. Let not your heart be troubled, neither let it be afraid. You have heard me say to you I am going away and coming back to you. If you loved Me, you would rejoice because I said I am going to the Father, for My Father is greater than I. And now I have told you before it comes, that when it does come to pass, you may believe. (John 14:23–29)

Jesus also said, "These things I have spoken to you, that in Me you may have peace. In the world you will have tribulation; but be of good cheer, I have overcome the world" (John 16:33).

Jesus Healed the Sick and Raised the Dead

Jesus healed the sick. Here we read about Jesus healing a twelve-year-old girl and a woman who was sick for twelve year with an issue of blood:

> And behold, there came a man named Jairus, and he was a ruler of the synagogue. And he fell down at Jesus' feet and begged Him to come to his house, for he had an only daughter about twelve years of age, and she was dying. But as He went, the multitudes thronged Him. Now a woman, having a flow of blood for twelve years, who had spent all her livelihood on physicians and could not be healed by any, came from behind and touched the border of His garment. And immediately her flow of blood stopped. And Jesus said, "Who touched Me?" When all denied it, Peter and those with him said, "Master, the multitudes throng You and press You and You say, who touched Me." But Jesus

said, "Somebody touched Me, for I perceived power going out from Me." Now when the woman saw that she was not hidden, she came trembling; and falling down before Him, she declared to Him in the presence of all the people the reason she had touched Him and how she was healed immediately. And He said to her, "Daughter, be of good cheer, your faith has made you well. Go in peace." While He was still speaking, someone came from the ruler of the synagogue's house, saying to him, "Your daughter is dead. Do not trouble the Teacher." But when Jesus heard it, He answered him, saying, Do not be afraid, only believe and she will be made well." When He came into the house, He permitted no one to go in except Peter, James and John, and the father and mother of the girl. Now all wept and mourned for her, but He said, "Do not weep; she is not dead, but sleeping." And they laughed Him to scorn, knowing that she was dead. But He put them all out, took her by the hand and called saying, "Little girl, arise." Then her spirit returned, and she arose immediately. And He commanded that she be given something to eat. And her parents were astonished, but He charged them to tell no one what had happened. (Luke 8:41–56)

The large crowd around Jesus did not deter the woman with an issue of blood. With immense faith and deep conviction, she touched the hem of His garment and was instantly made whole. Nothing goes unnoticed by Jesus. Right away Jesus noticed that someone had touched His clothes, and by the simple act of faith, she was made whole. She didn't even talk to Jesus and ask Him to heal her. Jesus didn't talk to her either, but the simple act of faith got the desired results.

Jesus notices everything. He is always ready to help. He is ever ready to perform miracles. He is never "too busy" for anyone. All we need is faith. When we pray and ask in faith, we receive miracles.

Here is one instance when Jesus raised a man who was dead:

Now a certain man was sick, Lazarus of Bethany, the town of Mary and her sister Martha. It was that Mary who anointed the Lord with fragrant oil and wiped His feet with her hair, whose brother Lazarus was sick. Therefore the sisters sent to Him, saying, "Lord, behold, he whom You love is sick." When Jesus heard that, He said, "This sickness is not unto death, but for the glory of God that the Son of God may be glorified through it." Now Jesus loved Martha and her sister and Lazarus. So, when He heard that he was sick, He stayed two more days in the place where He was. Then after this He said to the disciples, "Let us go to Judea again." The disciples said to Him, "Rabbi, lately the Jews sought to stone You, and are You going there again?" Jesus answered, "Are there not twelve hours in the day? If anyone walks in the day, he does not stumble, because he sees the light of this world. But if one walks in the night, he stumbles, because the light is not in him." These things He said and after that He said to them, "Our friend Lazarus sleeps, but I go that I may wake him up." Then His disciples said, "Lord if he sleeps he will get well." However, Jesus spoke of his death, but they thought He was speaking about taking rest in sleep. Then Jesus said to them plainly, "Lazarus is dead. And I am glad for your sakes that I was not there, that you may believe. Nevertheless let us go to him." So when Jesus came, He found that he had already been in the tomb four days. Now Bethany was near Jerusalem, about two miles away. And many of the Jews had joined the women around Martha and Mary, to comfort them concerning their brother. Then Martha, as soon as she heard that Jesus was coming, went and met Him, but Mary was sitting in the house. Then Martha said to Jesus, "Lord, if You had been here, my brother would not have died. But even now I know that whatever You ask of God, God will give You." Jesus said to her, "Your brother will rise again." Martha said to Him, "I know that he will rise again in the resurrection at the last day." Jesus said to her, "I am the resurrection and the life. He who believes in Me, though he may die he shall live. And whoever lives and believes in Me shall never die. Do you believe this?" She said to Him, "Yes Lord, I believe that You are the Christ, the Son of God, who is to come into the world". And when she had said these things, she went her way and secretly called Mary her sister, saying, "The Teacher has come and is calling for you." As soon as she heard that, she arose quickly and came to Him. Now Jesus had not yet come into the town, but was in the place where Martha met Him. Then the Jews who were with her in the house, and comforting her, when they saw that Mary rose up quickly and sent out, followed her, saying, "She is going to the tomb to weep there." Then, when Mary came where Jesus was, and saw Him, she fell down at His feet, saying to Him, "Lord, if You had been here, my brother would not have died." Therefore, when Jesus saw her weeping, and the Jews who came with her weeping, He groaned in the spirit and was troubled. And He said, "Where have you laid him?" They said to Him, "Lord, come and see." Jesus wept. Then the Jews said, "See how He loved him!" And some of them said, "Could not this Man who opened the eyes of the blind, also have kept this man from dying?" Then Jesus, again groaning in Himself came to the tomb. It was a cave, and a stone lay against it. Jesus said, "Take away the stone." Martha, the sister of him who was dead, said to Him, "Lord, by this time there is a stench, for he has been dead four days. Jesus said to her, "Did I not say to you that if you would believe you would see the glory of God?" Then they took away the stone from the place where the dead man was lying. And Jesus lifted His eyes and said, "Father, I thank You that You have heard Me. And I know that You always hear Me, but because of the people who are standing by I said this, that they may believe that You sent Me." Now when He had said these things, He cried with a loud voice, "Lazarus, come forth! And he who had died came out bound hand and foot with grave clothes, and his face was wrapped with a cloth. Jesus said to them, loose him, and let him go." (John 11:1-15, 17–44)

In the hopes that Jesus would heal Lazarus, Mary and Martha sent Him word that their brother was sick. Jesus waited a few days, and Lazarus died. Mary and Martha were expecting Jesus to come and heal their brother, but Jesus had other plans for Lazarus. He wanted to resurrect Lazarus, rather than heal him. Many times we ask Him with the expectation that He will do what we've asked for, but sometimes His answer comes in a different form. Jesus is Sovereign. He carries out His divine will. His answer is always in the form, which is best for us. While demonstrating His power over death Jesus said these comforting words, "I am the resurrection and the life. He who believes in Me, though he may die he shall live. And whoever lives and believes in Me shall never die" (John 11:25–26).

Chapter 5

The Teachings of Jesus

Jesus is considered the greatest teacher ever. His teachings are unique and revolutionary. He taught on different aspects concerning human behavior, morality, law, love, prayer, wealth, judging, fasting, the true way into the kingdom, the golden rule, and more. He said so much on different topics that volumes could be written just on what He said and taught while He was on this earth.

Jesus raised the standard of morality to an all time high. He said, "Be holy, for I am holy" (1 Peter 1:16).

"Pursue peace with all men, and holiness, without which no one will see the Lord" (Hebrews 12:14).

In this chapter we will touch on a few of His teachings, which are self-explanatory and hardly need elaboration.

Murder

Jesus said, "You have heard that it was said to those of old, 'you shall not murder,' and whoever murders will be in danger of the judgment. But I say to you that whoever is angry with his brother without a cause shall be in danger of the judgment. And whoever says to his brother, 'Raca' shall be in danger of the council. But whoever says, 'you fool' shall be in danger of hell fire. Therefore if you bring your gift to the altar, and there remember that your brother has something against you, leave your gift there before the altar, and go your way. First be reconciled to your brother, and then come and offer your gift." (Matthew 5:21–24)

God desires purity of heart. We cannot approach the throne of grace with malice in our hearts. Here the word *brother* means anyone with whom we may be angry or have done wrong to. Our gift at the altar will not be pleasing to God unless we reconcile with everyone.

Adultery

"You have heard that it was said to those, 'you shall not commit adultery.' But I say to you that whoever looks at a woman to lust for her has already committed adultery with her in his heart. And if your right eye causes you to sin, pluck it out and cast it from you; for it is more profitable for you that one of your members perish, than for your whole body to be cast into hell." Matthew 5: 27-29

Divorce

"Furthermore it has been said, whoever divorces his wife, let him give her a certificate of divorce. But I say to you, that whoever divorces his wife for any reason except sexual immorality, causes her to commit adultery; and whoever marries a woman who is divorced commits adultery." (Matthew 5:31–32)

Oaths

"Again you have heard that it was said to those of old, you shall not swear falsely but shall perform your oaths to the Lord. But I say to you, do not swear at all: neither by heaven, for it is God's throne; nor by the earth, for it is his footstool; nor by Jerusalem, for it is the city of the great King. Nor shall you swear by your head because you cannot make one hair white or black. But let your 'yes' be 'yes' and your 'no,' 'no'. For whatever is more than these is from the evil one." Matthew 5: 33-37

Retaliation

"You have heard that it was said, 'an eye for an eye and a tooth for a tooth.' But I tell you not to resist an evil person. But whoever slaps you on your right cheek, turn the other to him also. If anyone wants to sue you and take away your tunic, let him have your cloak also. And whoever compels you to go one mile, go with him two. Give to him who asks you, and from him who wants to borrow from you do not turn away." Matthew 5: 38-42

Love

"You have heard that it was said, 'you shall love your neighbor and hate your enemy.' But I say to you, love your enemies, bless those who curse you, do good to those who hate you, and pray for those who spitefully use you and persecute you, that you may be sons of your Father in heaven; for He makes His sun rise on the evil and on the good, and sends rain on the just and on the unjust. For if you love those who love you, what reward have you? Do not even the tax collectors do the same? And if you greet your brethren only, what do you do more than others? Do not even the tax collectors do so? Therefore, you shall be perfect just as your Father in heaven is perfect." (Matthew 5: 43-48)

It seems not only very hard, but even impossible to act on Jesus' teachings. From the natural and worldly point of view, none of us can love our enemies in our own strength, so how can we act on Jesus' teaching of 'love your enemies'? The answer is, we can love our enemies only in God's strength and with the help of the Holy Spirit, Who indwells every "born again" person. Therefore, Jesus said, "You must be born again."

When a person is born again, the Holy Spirit lives in him or her and helps that person to lead a pure and holy life. The Bible tells us that God is Spirit and all-holy. God made us in His image and likeness, so we have to acquire His attributes of love and purity. We are required to walk and act in the spirit realm and to lead a pure and holy life—without which we cannot see God.

What Defiles a Man?

Jesus said, "Not what goes into the mouth defiles a man; but what comes out of the mouth, this defiles a man." Matthew 15: 11. "Then Peter answered an said to Him, "Explain this parable to us." So Jesus said, "Are you also still without understanding? Do you not yet understand that whatever enters the mouth goes into the stomach and is eliminated? But those things which proceed out of the mouth come from the heart, and they defile a man. For out of the heart proceed evil thoughts, murders, adulteries, fornications, thefts, false witness, blasphemies. These are the things which defile a man, but to eat with unwashed hands does not defile a man." (Matthew 15: 15–20)

Forgiveness

Then Peter came to Him and said, "Lord, how often shall my brother sin against me, and I forgive him? Up to seven times?" Jesus said to him, "I do not say to you, up to seven times, but up to seventy times seven.' Therefore the kingdom of heaven is like a certain king who wanted to settle accounts with his servants. And when he had begun to settle accounts, one was brought to him who owed him ten thousand talents. But as he was not able to pay, his master commanded that he be sold, with his wife and children and all that he had, and that payment be made. The servant therefore fell down before him, saying, 'Master, have patience with me, and I will pay you all.' Then the master of that servant was moved with compassion, released him, and forgave him the debt. But that servant went out and found one of his fellow servants who owned him a hundred denarii; and he laid hands on him and took him by the throat, saying, 'Pay me what you owe!' So His fellow servant fell down at his feet and begged him, saying, 'Have patience with me, and I will pay you all.' And he would not, but went and threw him into prison till he should pay the debt. So when his fellow servants saw what had been done, they were very grieved, and came and told their master all that had been done. Then his master, after he had called him, said to him, 'You wicked servant! I forgave you all that debt because you begged me. Should you not also have had compassion on your fellow servant, just as I had pity on you?' And his master was angry and delivered him to the torturers until he should pay all that was due to him. So My heavenly Father also will do to you if each of you, from his heart, does not forgive his brother his trespasses." (Matthew 18:21–35)

Jesus' followers are required to forgive those who have wronged them. Jesus died for the sins of all humankind. He forgives sins of all who go to Him and repent. Therefore, the redeemed of the Lord are left with no choice but to forgive those who have wronged them. In our own strength, we cannot forgive anyone who has wronged us. We can do so only with the help of the Holy Spirit.

Charitable Deeds

"Take heed that you do not do your charitable deeds before men, to be seen by them. Otherwise you have no reward from your Father in heaven. Therefore, when you do a charitable deed, do not sound a trumpet before you as the hypocrites do in the synagogues and in the streets, that they may have glory from men. Assuredly, I say to you, they have their reward. But when you do a charitable deed, do not let your left hand know what your right hand is doing, that your charitable deed may be in secret; and your Father who sees in secret will Himself reward you openly." Matthew 6: 1-4

Prayer

"And when you pray, you shall not be as like the hypocrites. For they love to pray standing in the synagogues and on the corners of the streets, that they may be seen by men. Assuredly, I say to you, they have their reward. But you, when you pray, go into your room and when you have shut your door, pray to your Father who is in the secret place, and your Father who sees in secret will reward you openly. But when you pray do not use vain repetitions as the heathen do. For they think that they will be heard for their many words. Therefore do not be like them. For your Father knows the things you have need of before you ask Him. In this manner, therefore, pray: Our Father in heaven, hallowed be Your name. Your kingdom come. Your will be done on earth as it is in heaven. Give us this day our daily bread. And forgive us our debts, as we forgive our debtors. And do not lead us into temptation, but deliver us from the evil one. For Yours is the kingdom and the power and the glory forever. Amen. For if you forgive men their trespasses, your heavenly Father will also forgive you. But if you do not forgive men their trespasses, neither will your Father forgive your trespasses." Matthew 6: 5-15

Fasting

"Moreover, when you fast, do not be like the hypocrites, with a sad countenance. For they disfigure their faces that they may appear to men to be fasting. Assuredly, I say to you, they have their reward. But you, when you fast, anoint your head and wash your face, so that you do not appear to men to be fasting, but to your Father who is in the secret place; and your Father who sees in secret will reward you openly." Matthew 6: 16-18

Laying Up Treasures in Heaven

"Do not lay up for yourselves treasures on earth, where moth and rust destroy and where thieves break in and steal; but lay up for yourselves treasures in heaven, where neither moth nor rust destroys and where thieves do not break in and steal. For where your treasure is, there your heart will be also. The lamp of the body is the eye. If therefore your eye is good, your whole body will be full of light. But if your eye is bad, your whole body will be full of darkness. If therefore the light that is in you is darkness, how great is that darkness! No one can serve two masters; for either he will hate the one and love the other, or else he will be loyal to the one and despise the other. You cannot serve God and mammon. Therefore I say to you, do not worry about your life, what you will eat or what you will put on. Is not life more than food and the body more than clothing? Look at the birds of the air, for they neither sow nor reap nor gather into barns, yet your heavenly Father feeds them. Are you not of more value than they? Which of you by worrying can add one cubit to his stature? So why do you worry about clothing? Consider the lilies of the field, how they grow: they neither toil nor spin; and yet I say to you that even Solomon in all his glory was not arrayed like one of these. Now if God so clothes the grass of the field, which today is, and tomorrow is thrown into the oven, will He not much more clothe you, o you of little faith? Therefore do not worry saying, 'what shall we eat?' or what shall we drink? Or 'what shall we wear?' For after all these things the Gentiles seek. For your heavenly Father knows that you need all these things. But seek first the kingdom of God and His righteousness, and all these things shall be added to you. Therefore do not worry about tomorrow, for tomorrow will worry about its own things. Sufficient for the day is its own trouble." (Matthew 6:19–34)

Judging Others

"Judge not, that you be not judged. For with what judgment you judge, you will be judged; and with the same measure you use, it will be measured back to you. And why do you look at the spec in your brother's eye, but do not consider the plank in your own eye? Or how can you say to your brother, 'let me remove the speck out of your eye; and look, a plank is in your own eye? Hypocrite! First remove the plank from your own eye, and then you will see clearly to remove the speck out of your brother's eye. Do not give what is holy to the dogs; nor cast your pearls before swine, lest they trample them under their feet, and turn and tear you in pieces." (Matthew 7:1–6)

God Knows Our Needs

"Ask and it will be given to you; seek and you will find; knock and it will be opened to you. For everyone who asks receives, and he who seeks finds, and to him who knocks it will be opened. Or what man is there among you who, if his son asks for bread, will give him a stone? Or if he asks for a fish, will he give him a serpent? If you then, being evil know how to give good gifts to your children, how much more will your Father who is in heaven give good things to those who ask Him!" (Matthew 7:7–11)

The Golden Rule

"Whatever you want men to do to you do also to them, for this is the law of the prophets." (Matthew 7:12)

Narrow And Wide Gate

"Enter by the narrow gate; for wide is the gate and broad is the way that leads to destruction, and there are many who go in by it. Because narrow is the gate and difficult is the way which leads to life, and there are few who find it. Beware of false prophets, who come to you in sheep's clothing, but inwardly they are ravenous wolves. You will know them by their fruits. Do men gather grapes from thornbushes or figs from thistles? Even so, every good tree bears good fruit, but a bad tree bears bad fruit. A good tree cannot bear bad fruit, nor can a bad tree bear good fruit. Every tree that does not bear good fruit is cut down and thrown into the fire. Therefore by their fruits you will know them." (Matthew 7:13–20)

Fear God, Not Men

"Do not fear those who kill the body but cannot kill the soul. But rather fear Him who is able to destroy both soul and body in hell. Are not two sparrows sold for a copper coin? And not one of them falls to the ground apart from your Father's will. But the very hairs of your head are all numbered. Do not fear therefore; you are of more value than many sparrows. Therefore whoever confesses Me before men, him I will also confess before My Father who is in heaven. But whoever denies Me before men, him I will also deny before My Father who is in heaven. Do not think that I came to bring peace on earth. I did not come to bring peace but a sword. For I have come to set a man against his father, a daughter against her mother, and a daughter-in-law against her mother-in-law. And a man's foes will be those of his own household. He who loves father or mother more than Me is not worthy of Me. And he who loves son or daughter more than Me is not worthy of Me. And he who does not take his cross and follow after Me is not worthy of Me. He who finds his life will lose it, and he who loses his life for My sake will find it. He who receives you receives Me, and he who receives Me receives Him who sent Me. He who receives a prophet in the name of a prophet shall receive a prophet's reward. And he who receives a righteous man in the name of a righteous man shall receive a righteous man's reward. And whoever gives one of these little ones only a cup of cold water in the name of a disciple, assuredly, I say to you, he shall by no means lose his reward." (Matthew 10:28–42)

Instruction about Humility

"At that time the disciples came to Jesus, saying, "Who then is greatest in the kingdom of heaven? And Jesus called a little child to Him, set him in the midst of them, and said, 'Assuredly, I say to you, unless you are converted and become as little children, you will by no means enter the kingdom of heaven. Therefore whoever humbles him self as this little child is the greatest in the kingdom of heaven, and whoever receives one little child like this in My name receives Me. But whoever causes one of these little ones who believe in Me to sin, it would be better for him if a millstone were hung around his neck, and he were drowned in the depth of the sea. Woe to the world because of offenses! For offenses must come, but woe to that man by whom the offense comes. And if your hand or foot causes you to sin, cut it off and cast it from you. It is better for you to enter into life lame or maimed, rather than having two hands or two feet, to be cast into the everlasting fire. And if your eye causes you to sin, pluck it out and cast it from you. It is better for you to enter into life with one eye, rather than having two eyes, to be cast into hell fire. Take heed that you do not despise one of these little ones, for I say to you that in heaven their angels always see the face of My Father who is in heaven." (Matthew 18:1–10)

Great Commandment

Then one of the, a lawyer, asked Him a question, testing Him and saying, "Teacher, which is the great command-ment in the law?" Jesus said to him, "You shall love the Lord your God with all your heart, with all your soul, and with all your mind. This is the first and great commandment. And the second is like it: 'You shall love your neighbor as yourself.' On these two commandments hang all the Law and the prophets." (Matthew 22:35–40)

Jesus Witnesses to Nicodemus

There was a man of the Pharisees named Nicodemus, a ruler of the Jews. This man came to Jesus by night and said to Him, "Rabbi, we know that You are a teacher come from God; for no one can do these signs that You do unless God is with him." Jesus answered and said to him, "Most assuredly, I say to you, unless one is born again, he cannot see the kingdom of God." Nicodemus said to Him, "How can a man be born when he is old? Can he enter a second time into his mother's womb and be born?" Jesus answered. "Most assuredly, I say to you, unless one is born of water and the Spirit, he cannot enter the kingdom of God. That which is born of the flesh is flesh, and that which is born of the Spirit is spirit. Do not marvel that I said to you, you must be born again. The wind blows where it wishes, and you hear the sound of it, but cannot tell where it comes from and where it goes. So is everyone who is born of the Spirit." Nicodemus answered and said to Him, "How can these things be?" Jesus answered and said to him, "Are you the teacher of Israel, and do not know these things? Most assuredly, I say to you, We speak what We know and testify what We have seen, and you do not receive Our witness. If I have told you earthly things and you do not believe, how will you believe if I tell you heavenly things? No one has ascended to heaven but He who came down from heaven, that is, the Son of Man who is in heaven. And as Moses lifted up the serpent in the wilderness, even so must the Son of Man be lifted up, that whoever believes in Him should not perish but have eternal life. For God so loved the world that He gave His only begotten Son, that whoever believes in Him should not perish but have everlasting life. For God did not send His Son into the world to condemn the world, but that the world through Him might be saved. He who believes in Him is not condemned; but he who does not believe is condemned already, because he has not believed in the name of the only begotten Son of God. And this is the condemnation, that the light has come into the world, and men loved darkness rather than light, because their deeds were evil. For everyone practicing evil hates the light and does not come to the light, lest his deeds should be exposed. But he who does the truth comes to the light, that his deeds may be clearly seen, that they have been 'done in God.'" (John 3:1–21)

The Beatitudes

The word *beatitude* is from the Latin word *beautitudines*. *Beatus* means happy, fortunate, or blissful. In his gospel, Matthew narrates the Sermon on the Mount, part of which we call the Beatitudes. Jesus Christ gave us eight beatitudes to show us a way of life that leads to eternity in the kingdom of heaven.

"Blessed are the poor in spirit, for theirs is the kingdom of heaven. Blessed are those who mourn, for they shall be comforted. Blessed are the meek, for they shall inherit the earth. Blessed are those who hunger and thirst for righteousness, for they shall be filled. Blessed are the merciful, for they shall obtain mercy. Blessed are the pure in heart, for they shall see God. Blessed are the peacemakers for they shall be called sons of God. Blessed are those who are persecuted for righteousness' sake, for theirs is the kingdom of heaven. Blessed are you when they revile and persecute you, and say all kinds of evil against you falsely for My sake, rejoice and be exceedingly glad, for great is your reward in heaven, for so they persecuted the prophets who were before you." (Matthew 5:3-12)

We see in these beatitudes a message of humility, charity, and brotherly love. We also see that Jesus wants to change our inner being. Through the Beatitudes, Jesus teaches us virtues that ultimately lead to reward. The Beatitudes promise us not only salvation in this world, but also reward in the next. They also provide peace in the midst of our trials and tribulation on this earth. The opposite of happiness is misery; we all know that means painful sufferings.

Let's look at a few of the beatitudes more closely.

Blessed are the poor in spirit. "Poor in spirit" refers to those who are humble. Simply put, the humble and not the proud will inherit the kingdom of heaven. Humility brings repentance and inner peace as well as an awareness of our need to do the will of God. The opposite of humility is pride, which leads to anger, misery, and other vices. Pride is what causes human conflicts, struggles, and wars.

Blessed are those who mourn, for they shall be comforted. Those who believe in Jesus find peace that passes all understanding, and their hearts and minds find rest in Him. Here's what Jesus said to those who mourn: "These things I have spoken to you, that in Me you may have peace. In the world you will have tribulation; but be of good cheer, I have overcome the world" (John 16:33). Jesus also said, "Peace I leave with you, My peace I give to you; not as the world gives do I give to you. Let not your heart be troubled, neither let it be afraid"(John 14:27).

Blessed are the meek, for they shall inherit the earth. The word *meek* means patient, gentle, mild, compassionate, and kind. Meek does not mean "weak." Being meek is actually being strong. Jesus, who was meek and mild Himself, said, "Take My yoke upon you and learn from Me, for I am gentle and lowly in heart, and you will find rest for your souls. For My yoke is easy and My burden is light" (Matthew 11:29-30). Jesus was meek; but in no way He was weak. Meekness means submission to the will of God . Those who are weak take the yoke of Jesus on themselves and learn from Him; as they do this, they find peace, rest, and comfort in this world. The Word of God says, "You will keep him in perfect peace, whose mind is stayed on You, because he trusts in You" (Isaiah 26:3).

Chapter 6

The Second Coming of Jesus

Jesus' Ascension into Heaven

After living and completing His mission on earth, Jesus ascended into heaven. Before his ascension He comforted His disciples and followers with these words: "Let not your heart be troubled; you believe in God, believe also in Me. In My Father's house are many mansions; if it were not so, I would have told you. I go to prepare a place for you. And if I go and prepare a place for you, I will come again and receive you to Myself; that where I am, there you may be also. And where I go you know, and the way you know" (John 14:1–4).

Jesus' disciples were saddened that He was leaving them, but He assured them that He would not leave them alone and promised that He would send the Holy Spirit Who would guide them into all truth.

"But you shall receive power when the Holy Spirit has come upon you; and you shall be witnesses to Me in Jerusalem, and in all Judea and Samaria, and to the end of the earth." Now when He had spoken these things, while they watched, He was taken up, and a cloud received Him out of their sight. And while they looked steadfastly toward heaven as He went up, behold, two men stood by them in white apparel, who also said, "Men of Galilee why do you stand gazing up into heaven? This same Jesus, who was taken up from you into heaven, will so come in like manner as you saw Him go into heaven." (Acts 1:8–11).

There are more than three hundred prophecies about Jesus in Scripture. Prophecies concerning His birth, crucifixion, resurrection, and ascension have all been fulfilled. Let's look at some of the prophecies concerning His second coming:

When He came the first time, very few people knew of the fact, but when He comes the second time, every eye will see Him, including those who crucified and pierced Him. John the evangelist prophesied, "Behold, He is coming with clouds, and every eye will see Him, and they also who pierced Him. And all the tribes of the earth will mourn because of Him" (Revelation 1:7).

Also, everyone will kneel before Him, and everyone will say that Jesus Christ is Lord. "For it is written: 'As I live,' says the Lord, 'every knee shall bow to Me, and every tongue shall confess to God" (Romans 14:11).

Another Scripture saith, "They shall look on Him whom they pierced." (John 19:37)

Jesus served God and humanity while He was on this earth, therefore God has exalted Him that at the name of Jesus every knee will bow and every tongue will confess that Jesus is Lord.

It is written, "Let this mind be in you which was also in Christ Jesus, who, being in the form of God, did not consider it robbery to be equal with God, but made Himself of no reputation, taking the form of a servant, and coming in the likeness of men. And being found in appearance as a man, He humbled Himself and became obedient to the point of death, even the death of the cross. Therefore

God also has highly exalted Him and given Him the name which is above every name, that at the name of Jesus every knee should bow, of those in heaven, and of those on earth, and of those under the earth, and that every tongue should confess that Jesus Christ is Lord, to the glory of God the Father." (Philippians 2:5–11)

Before Jesus went into heaven, He promised He would come again, and gave many signs of His second coming to fore warn His followers. He said, "And you will see the Son of Man sitting at the right hand of the Power, and coming with the clouds of heaven" (Mark 14:62).

He further said, "Immediately after the tribulation of those days the sun will be darkened, and the moon will not give its light; the stars will fall from heaven, and the powers of the heavens will be shaken. Then the sign of the Son of Man will appear in heaven, and then all the tribes of the earth will mourn, and they will see the Son of Man coming on the clouds of heaven with power and great glory. And He will send His angels with a great sound of a trumpet, and they will gather together His elect from the four winds, from one end of heaven to the other." (Matthew 24:29–31)

"And there will be signs in the sun, in the moon, and in the stars; and on the earth distress of nations, with perplexity, the sea and the waves roaring; men's hearts failing them from fear and the expectation of those things which are coming on the earth, for the powers of heaven will be shaken. Then they will see the Son of Man coming in a cloud with power and great glory. Now when these things begin to happen, look up and lift up your heads, because your redemption draws near." And He spoke to them in a parable: "Look at the fig tree, and all the trees. When they are already budding, you see and know for yourselves that summer is now near. So you, likewise, when you see these things happening, know that the kingdom of God is near. Assuredly, I say to you, this generation will by no means pass away till all things are fulfilled. Heaven and earth will pass away, but My words will by no means pass away. But take heed to your selves, lest your hearts be weighed down with carousing, drunkenness, and cares of this life, and that Day come on you unexpectedly. For it will come as a snare on all those who dwell on the face of the whole earth. Watch therefore, and pray always that you may be counted worthy to escape all these things that will come to pass, and to stand before the Son of Man." (Luke 21:25–36)

The signs all around me remind me that I must be ready so I may be counted worthy to meet Him when He comes.

The day of His second coming is approaching fast. All signs are pointing towards this important and glorious event. It is written in the Holy Bible that when He appears on this earth the second time, every knee will bow before Him and every tongue will confess that Jesus Christ is Lord. I choose to bow my knee before Him now and confess that Jesus Christ is my Lord and Savior, because it is of utmost importance that I accept Him as my Lord and Savior while I am still alive, so He finds me worthy to spend eternity with Him. Jesus behooves all of us to guard our souls, which fact needs hardly be over emphasized.

Jesus said, "Whoever desires to come after Me, let him deny himself, and take up his cross, and follow Me. For whoever desires to save his life will lose it, but whoever loses his life for My sake and the gospel's will save it. For what will it profit a man if he gains the whole world, and loses his own soul? Or what will a man give in exchange for his soul? For whoever is ashamed of Me and My words in this adulterous and sinful generation, of him the Son of Man also will be ashamed when He comes in the glory of His Father with the Holy angels." (Mark 8:34–38)

And the New Testament is full of references to it. Here are just two more:

"And as it is appointed for men to die once, but after this the judgment, so Christ was offered once to bear the sins of many. To those who eagerly wait for Him He will appear a second time, apart from sin, for salvation." (Hebrews 9:27–28)

But I do not want you to be ignorant, brethren, concerning those who have fallen asleep, lest you sorrow as others who have no hope. For if we believe that Jesus died and rose again, even so God will bring with Him those who sleep in Jesus. For this we say to you by the word of the Lord, that we who are alive and remain until the coming of the Lord will by no means precede those who are asleep. For the Lord Himself will descend from heaven with a shout, with the voice of an archangel, and with the trumpet of God. And the dead in Christ will rise first. Then we who are alive and remain shall be caught up together with them in the clouds to meet the Lord in the air. And thus we shall always be with the Lord. (1 Thessalonians 4:13–17)

He Will Come as the King

When He comes again, Jesus will come as the triumphant King to rule. When He first came, He was born in a stable and willingly lived a very humble life, serving humanity. Very few people knew about His birth, but when He comes the second time, He will come with great splendor, accompanied by His angels. Matthew wrote in his Gospel, "For as the lightning comes from the east and flashes to the west, so also will the coming of the Son of Man be" (Matthew 24:27).

The "Seed" of the woman has crushed the serpent's head. Satan has been overthrown, and the earth's rightful owner has taken control. He governs it with truth and grace and justice. The head that once wore a crown of thorns now wears the crown of glory. The hand that was once pierced will hold the scepter. The feet that were once pierced will mount the throne. The kingdoms of this world are become the kingdoms of our Lord and of His Christ. He shall reign forever and ever as the King of kings and the Lord of lords . What was cursed because of sin will be restored to its original beauty.

He Will Judge and Reward Each According to His or Her Works.

Jesus will judge and reward everyone when He returns to this earth. In Acts 17: 31 it is written, "Because He has appointed a day on which He will judge the world in righteousness by the Man whom He has ordained. He has given assurance of this to all by raising Him from the dead".

When He first came to this earth, Jesus came as a lamb to be slaughtered; He came as the suffering Messiah. But when He comes the second time, He will come as the conquering Messiah. He is coming to judge the world, as he said, "For the Father judges no one, but has committed all judgment to the Son, that all should honor the Son just as they honor the Father. He who does not honor the Son does not honor the Father who sent Him. Most assuredly, I say to you, he who hears My word and believes in Him who sent Me has everlasting life, and shall not come into judgment, but has passed from death into life" (John 5:22–24).

When Jesus comes the second time, He will reward everyone according to his or her works.

"When the Son of Man comes in His glory, and all the holy angels with Him, then He will sit on the throne of His glory. All the nations will be gathered before Him, and He will separate them one from another, as a shepherd divides his sheep from the goats. And He will set the sheep on His right hand, but the goats on the left. Then the King will say to those on His right hand, 'Come, you blessed of My Father, inherit the kingdom prepared for you from the foundation of the world: for I was hungry and you gave Me food; I was thirsty and you gave Me drink; I was a stranger and you took Me in; I was naked and you clothed Me; I was sick and you visited Me; I was in prison and you came to Me.' Then the righteous will answer Him, saying, 'Lord, when did we see You hungry and feed You, or thirsty and give You drink? When did we see You a stranger and take You in, or naked and clothe you? Or when did we see You sick, or in prison, and come to You?' And the King will answer and say to them, 'Assuredly, I say to you, inasmuch as you did it to one of the least of these My brethren, you did it to me.' Then He will also say to those on the left hand, 'Depart from Me, you cursed, into the everlasting fire prepared for the devil and his angels: for I was hungry and you gave Me no food; I was thirsty and you gave Me no drink; I was a stranger and you did not take Me in, naked and you did not clothe Me, sick and in prison and you did not visit Me.' Then they also will answer Him, saying, 'Lord, when did we see You hungry or thirsty or a stranger or naked or sick or in prison, and did not minister to You?' Then He will answer them, saying, 'Assuredly, I say to you, inasmuch as you did not do it to one of the least of these, you did not do it to Me.' And these will go away into everlasting punishment, but the righteous into eternal life." (Matthew 25:31–46)

"For the Son of Man will come in the glory of His Father with His angels, and then He will reward each according to his works." (Matthew 16:27)

"And behold, I am coming quickly, and My reward is with Me, to give to every one according to his work. I am the Alpha and the

Omega, the Beginning and the End, the First and the Last. Blessed
are those who do His commandments, that they may have the right
to the tree of life, and may enter through the gates into the city. But
outside are dogs and sorcerers and sexually immoral and murderers
and idolaters and whoever loves and practices a lie. I, Jesus, have
sent My angel to testify to you these things in the churches. I am
the Root and the Offspring of David, the Bright and Morning Star.
And the Spirit and the bride say, 'Come!' And let him who hears
say, 'Come! 'And let him who thirsts come. And whoever desires,
let him take the water of life freely." (Revelation 22:12–17)

When Is Jesus Coming?

"But of that day and hour no one knows, no, not even the angels
of heaven, but my Father only. But as the days of Noah were, so also
will the coming of the Son of Man be. For as in the days before
the flood they were eating and drinking, marrying and giving in
marriage, until the day that Noah entered the ark, and did not know
until the flood came and took them all away, so also will the coming
of the Son of Man be. Then two men will be in the field: one will be
taken and the other left. Two women will be grinding at the mill:
one will be taken and the other left. Watch therefore, for you do
not know what hour your Lord is coming. But know this, that if the
master of the house had known what hour the thief would come, he
would have watched and not allowed his house to be broken into.
Therefore you also be ready, for the Son of Man is coming at an hour
when you do not expect Him." (Matthew 24:36–44)

God wants us to be ready to receive Jesus and to be with Him.
"Watch, therefore, for you do not know what hour the Lord is coming. But know this, that if the master of the house had known what
hour the thief would come, he would have watched and not allowed

his house to be broken into. Therefore you also be ready for the Son of man is coming at an hour when you do not expect Him." Matthew 24: 42 – 44.

God wants us to be ready, because He loves us and does not want any to perish. He is faithful, merciful, and compassionate. He sent His Son Jesus Christ to save all humanity. Humanity has failed God miserably. God created humans and placed them in the garden of Eden. That was the age of innocence, and Adam and Eve disobeyed God. God gave laws through Moses, but this ended with people crucifying Christ.

Now we live under grace, yet humanity is still at war against God and His Christ. But thanks again to God, for "as many as received Him, to them He gave the right to become children of God, to those who believe in His name: who were born, not of blood, nor of the will of the flesh, nor of the will of man, but of God" (John 1:12–13).

The blood of Jesus Christ is the only hope and remedy to set humanity free from the old "Adam nature" with its inborn sin and guilt and from rebellion against God.

Chapter 7

Jesus the Prophet

A lot of titles have been fittingly ascribed to Jesus Christ. Here are just a few:

- Prophet (Deuteronomy 18:15, 18)
- Seed of the Woman (Genesis 3:15)
- The everlasting Father (Isaiah 9:6)
- The Lord of our righteousness (Jeremiah 23:6)
- Son of God (Daniel 3:25)
- Son of Man (Daniel 7:13)
- Lamb of God (John 1:29)
- The Light of the world (John 8:12)
- The good Shepherd (John 10:11)
- The Way, the Truth, and the Life (John 14:6)
- The Rock (1 Corinthians 10:4)
- The Chief Cornerstone (Ephesians 2:20)
- Lord of lords (Revelation 19:16)
- The Morning Star (Revelation 22:16)

Jesus mainly occupied three offices: king, priest, and prophet. He talked about future events, telling His followers the signs of the end times. A prophet of God speaks what he receives from the Lord. He gives to people the message of God. He acts as the channel between God and people, and He reveals God's will to humanity. Jesus did all of these. While He was on this earth, He Himself carried the will of the Father: "Father, if it is Your will, remove this cup from Me; nevertheless not My will, but Yours, be done" (Luke 22:42).

Jesus revealed the Father. "All things have been delivered to Me by My Father, and no one knows the Son except the Father. Nor does anyone know the Father except the Son, and he to whom the Son wills to reveal Him" (Matthew 11:27).

Jesus spoke the things of the Father. "Then Jesus said to them, "When you lift up the Son of Man, then you will know that I am He and that I do nothing of Myself; but as My Father taught Me, I speak these things" (John 8:28).

Jesus refers to Himself as a prophet. "On that very day some Pharisees came, saying to Him, 'get out and depart from here, for Herod wants to kill you.' And He said to them, 'go tell that fox, behold, I cast out demons and perform cures today and tomorrow, and the third day I shall be perfected. Nevertheless I must journey today, tomorrow, and the day following; for it cannot be that a prophet should perish outside of Jerusalem" (Luke 13:32).

As a prophet, Jesus said a lot about the future of this world. Speaking about the end-time tribulation, he said,

> "Take heed that no one deceives you. For many will come in My name, saying, I am the Christ, and will deceive many. And you will hear of wars and rumors of wars. See that you are not troubled, for all these things must come to pass, but the end is not yet. For nation will rise against nation, and kingdom against kingdom. And there will be famines,

pestilences, and earthquakes in various places. All these are the beginning of sorrows. Then they will deliver you up to tribulation and kill you, and you will be hated by all nations for My name's sake. And then many will be offended, will betray one another, and will hate one another. Then many false prophets will rise up and deceive many. And because lawlessness will abound, the love of many will grow cold. But he who endures to the end shall be saved. And this gospel of the kingdom will be preached in all the world as a witness to all the nations, and then the end will come." (Matthew 24:4–14)

"For then there will be great tribulation, such as has not been since the beginning of the world until this time, no, nor ever shall be. And unless those days were shortened, no flesh would be saved; but for the elect's sake those days will be shortened. Then if anyone says to you, "Look, here is the Christ!" or "There!" do not believe it. For false christs and false prophets will arise and show great signs and wonders, so as to deceive, if possible, even the elect. See, I have told you beforehand. Therefore if they say to you, "Look He is in the desert!" do not go out; or "Look, He is in the inner rooms!" Do not believe. For as the lightning comes from the east and flashes to the west, so also will the coming of the Son of Man be. For wherever the carcass is, there the eagles will be gathered together. Immediately after the tribulation of those days the sun will be darkened, and the moon will not give its light; the stars will fall from heaven, and the powers of the heavens will be shaken. Then the sign of the Son of Man will appear in heaven, and then all the tribes of the earth will mourn and they will see the

Son of Man coming on the clouds of heaven with power and great glory. And He will send His angels with a great sound of a trumpet, and they will gather together His elect from the four winds, from one end of heaven to the other. Now learn this parable from the fig tree; when its branch has already become tender and puts forth leaves, you know that summer is near. So you also, when you see all these things, know that it is near, at the very doors." (Matthew 24:21–33)

Jesus requires us to pray and be ready for His second coming. To emphasize the importance of this, He told the parable of a wise and faithful servant:

Who then is a faithful and wise servant, whom his master made ruler over his household, to give them food in due season? Blessed is that servant whom his master, when he comes will find so doing. Assuredly, I say to you that he will make him ruler over all his goods. But if that evil servant says in his heart, My master is delaying his coming, and begins to beat his fellow servants, and to eat and drink with the drunkards, and the master of that servant will come on a day when he is not looking for him and at an hour that he is not aware of, and will cut him in two and appoint him his portion with the hypocrites. There shall be weeping and gnashing of teeth. (Matthew 24:45–51)

And there will be signs in the sun, in the moon, and in the stars; and on the earth distress of nations, with perplexity, the sea and the waves roaring; men's hearts failing them from fear and the expectation of those things which are coming on the earth, for the powers of heaven will be shaken. Then they will see the Son of Man coming in a cloud with power and great glory. (Luke 21:25–27)

In talking about His second coming, Jesus has given a road map to His followers so they are not caught unaware and unprepared. He wants them to be ready for His second coming. He named the events that would take place before He comes. He warned the faithful beforehand so they can prepare themselves and be ready for the glorious event of His majestic appearance. He said, "Now when these things begin to happen, look up and lift up your heads, because your redemption draws near" (Luke 21:28).

We live in the time between the first and second coming of Jesus Christ. The signs that will precede His coming are wars, blood in the streets, famines, earthquakes, roaring seas, and falling stars. All this will cause people to be frightened. There will be a complete panic. And in the midst of all this confusion, the Son of Man will appear with splendor, power, and heavenly glory. No one on this earth will miss this greatest event. Every eye will behold Him, including those who nailed Him to the cross and also those who pierced Him.

Jesus is coming as the triumphant King and the Lord of lords to judge and rule the world. When He first came, very few knew about His birth; but when He comes the second time, it will be magnificent—too big to miss. When He comes, He will finish what He started on this planet earth. He is coming to gather His saints and His martyrs.

Jesus warns us, saying, in essence, "Put your heads up; be alert; pray that you have strength to stand." He is bringing the kingdom of God and justice on earth. He is telling His followers not to give up, because their redemption is drawing near.

God's redemption is justice. A person who desires redemption wants the kingdom of God. When Jesus the King returns to this earth, He will bring His kingdom with Him and will reign with truth and grace. At last, His righteousness will fill the earth.

Jesus wants His believers to be on guard. He is telling them, "Don't let the worldly cares weigh you down. Stay alert. Stand up and raise your heads because the kingdom of heaven is coming." Every believer who believes in the kingdom of God must pray for those who are without much hope.

The signs and events that Jesus mentioned are unfolding right before our eyes with pinpoint accuracy. Let's just look around us. People have become haughty, proud, selfish, and hateful toward others. This is the result of much hatred and unrest in the human heart. We see wars and bloodshed in different parts of the world. To prove their supremacy and satiate their hunger to dominate, nations are trying to conquer and subdue other nations. There is turmoil, unrest, and bloodshed within many countries.

Like never before, we are witnessing floods, earthquakes, droughts, and tsunamis in different parts of the world. These calamities have always been there, but their frequency and ferocity are unparalleled in history. Followers of Jesus are hated, discriminated against, and killed in many nations; He warned us beforehand that this would happen. Jesus also warned against false prophets. Just as a tree is known by the fruit it bears, so we can also know a prophet by the fruit of his or her life.

Being the omniscient God, Jesus knows all. What He says comes to pass. Therefore, he said emphatically, "Heaven and earth will pass away, but My words will by no means pass away" (Matthew 24:35). These signs and these words should be enough to convince skeptics and cynics to repent of their sins and to accept Jesus as their Lord and Savior.

The gospel of the kingdom is being preached everywhere throughout the world through every media. Also, Jesus is appearing to many through dreams and visions in different parts of the world.

Today many people are very much afraid of the events that are taking place. Their hearts are failing because of fear. In these end times, knowledge has increased rapidly. Despite much advancement in science and technology, we have not been able to solve humanity's problems—if anything, our problems are increasing. There is no value for human life and safety. There is no security in the financial and business world.

Chapter 8

What Does Jesus
Require of You

"He has shown you, o man, what is good and what does the Lord require of you but to do justly, to love mercy, and to walk humbly with your God." Micah 6:8

These are three simple commands: Do justly, love mercy, and walk humbly with God. Their meaning is clear. To walk justly means to act on God's standards for right and wrong. It means that we should not do anything that is not in accordance with God's will. It means that we are required to use God's standards of right and wrong instead of our own.

The word 'just' here means 1. Fair handed, or impartial in judging. 2. Adhering to high moral standards. 3. Upright. 4. Honest and 5. legitimate.

So, what does Jesus require of us? "And you shall love the Lord your God with all your heart, with all your soul, with all your mind and with all your strength. This is the first commandment. And the second, like it, is this, you shall love your neighbor as yourself. There is no other commandment greater than these" (Mark 12:30–31).

We are to give God what is due Him and people what is due them. If we fail to do that, we are not just , because this is what the Lord God requires of us.

If I love God, I will try not to sin against Him knowingly. In the same way, if I love others, I will try not to sin against them willingly. When we accept Jesus Christ as our Lord and Savior, we become His property, because by dying on the cross for the sins of humankind, Jesus paid a price for our salvation. He purchased our salvation at a very high price.

> Do you not know that your bodies are members of Christ? Shall I then take the members of Christ and make them members of a harlot? Certainly not! Or do you not know that he who is joined to a harlot is one body with her? For the two, He says, shall become one flesh. But he who is joined to the Lord is one spirit with Him. Flee sexual immorality. Every sin that a man does is outside the body, but he who commits sexual immorality sins against his own body. Or do you not know that your body is the temple of the Holy Spirit who is in you, whom you have from God, and you are not your own? For you were bought at a price; therefore glorify God in your body and in your spirit, which are God's. (1 Corinthians 6:15–20)

Mercy is defined in this way: 1. Kind and compassionate treatment of an offender, adversary, prisoner, etc. Compassion, where severity is expected or deserved. 2. A disposition to be kind, forgiving, or helpful. 3. The power to show mercy or compassion. God demonstrates mercy and love toward sinful people. We do not deserve His mercy, but out of His love for us, God showed mercy. When Adam and Eve sinned, God could have annihilated them;

but He showed love and mercy to them. Then He sent the Savior Jesus Christ, who laid down His life willingly for our sins.

Mercy also means kindness, benevolence, and love. We are required to be willing to forgive the sins of others, because this is the nature of God. The true test is having to be kind to those who have wronged us. The prophet Micah said, "Who is a God like You, pardoning iniquity and passing over the transgression of the remnant of His heritage? He does not retain His anger forever, because He delights in mercy" (Micah 7:18). God has shown mercy to humanity. Therefore, it behooves us to show mercy to others.

We did not earn God's mercy. He bestowed it on us out of His love for us:

> Not by works of righteousness which we have done, but according to His mercy He saved us, through the washing of generation and renewing of the Holy Spirit, whom He poured out on us abundantly through Jesus Christ our Savior, that having been justified by His grace we should become heirs according to the hope of eternal life. This is a faithful saying, and these things I want you to affirm constantly, that those who have believed in God should be careful to maintain good works. These things are good and profitable to men. But avoid foolish disputes, genealogies, contentions, and strivings about the law, for they are unprofitable and useless. (Titus 3:5–9)

What does it mean to "walk humbly"? "Submit to God. Resist the devil and he will flee from you. Draw near to God and He will draw near to you. Cleanse your hands, you sinners; and purify your hearts, you double-minded" (James 4:6–8).

Without loving mercy and walking humbly, we would be slaves

to our sinful nature, succumbing to the habits of the flesh and not maintaining right relationship with Him and other people. God has rescued us and extended the perfect gift of salvation, and He commands us to extend that grace to others: "Likewise you younger people, submit yourselves to your elders. Yes, all of you be submissive to one another, and be clothed with humility, for God resists the proud, but gives grace to the humble. Therefore humble yourselves under the mighty hand of God, that He may exalt you in due time, casting all your care upon Him, for He cares for you" (1 Peter 5:5–7).

God hates the proud but loves the meek and humble. We draw near to God when we show humility, repentance, submission to His will, prayer and by serving Him. Jesus said, "Take My yoke upon you and learn from Me, for I am gentle and lowly in heart, and you will find rest for your souls. For My yoke is easy and My burden is light" (Matthew 12:29–30).

Jesus Commands Us to Repent of Sin.

- "Jesus began to preach and to say, "Repent for the kingdom of heaven is at hand" (Matthew 4:17).
- "Unless you repent you will all likewise perish" (Luke 13:3).
- "Repent therefore and be converted, that your sins may be blotted out, so that times of refreshing may come from the presence of the Lord" (Acts 3:19).
- "Truly, these times of ignorance God overlooked, but now commands all men everywhere to repent, because He has appointed a day on which He will judge the world in righteousness by the Man whom He has ordained. He has given assurance of this to all by raising Him from the dead" (Acts 17:30–31).

Believe and Be Baptized.

The command to believe is the basis of the gospel message.

- "God so loved the world that He gave His only begotten Son, that whoever believes in Him should not perish but have everlasting life" (John 3:16).
- "I said to you that you will die in your sins; for if you do not believe that I am He, you will die in your sins" (John 8:24).
- "And truly Jesus did many other signs in the presence of His disciples, which are not written in this book; but these are written that you may believe that Jesus is the Christ, the Son of God, and that believing you may have life in His name" (John 20:30).
- "Then Peter said to them, "Repent, and let every one of you be baptized in the name of Jesus Christ for the remission of sins; and you shall receive the gift of the Holy Spirit'" (Acts 2:38).
- "And he commanded them to be baptized in the name of the Lord" (Acts 10:48).
- "And now why are you waiting? Arise and be baptized, and wash away your sins calling on the name of the Lord" (Acts 22:16).

Become His Disciples.

- Jesus says, "Come to Me, all you who labor and are heavy laden, and I will give you rest. Take My yoke upon you and learn from Me, for I am gentle and lowly in heart, and you will find rest for your souls. For My yoke is easy and My burden is light" (Matthew 11:28–30).

- "Then Jesus came and spoke to them, saying, 'All authority has been given to Me in heaven and on earth. Go therefore and make disciples of all nations, baptizing them in the name of the Father and of the Son and of the Holy Spirit, teaching them to observe all things that I have commanded you; and lo, I am with you always, even to the end of the age'" (Matthew 28:18–20).

Be Faithful Until Death

Just as a seed, planted in good ground, grows, and brings forth much fruit, we are to bear much fruit and be grounded in God's Word until death, so on judgment day, He will say, "Well done, my good and faithful servant." Jesus taught through a parable about people who hear His Word and for a short time keep it, but then deviate from it. Those who hear His Word and keep it bear much fruit.

A sower went out to sow his seed. And as he sowed, some fell by the wayside; and it was trampled down, and the birds of the air devoured it. Some fell on rock; and as soon as it sprang up, it withered away because it lacked moisture. And some fell among thorns, and the thorns sprang up with it and choked it. But others fell on good ground, sprang up, and yielded a crop a hundredfold. Luke 8: 5-8.

"His disciples asked Him to explain this parable and Jesus said, "To you it has been given to know the mysteries of the kingdom of God, but to the rest it is given in parables, that seeing they may not see and hearing they may not understand. Now the parable is this: The seed is the word of God. Those by the wayside are the ones who hear; then the devil comes and takes away the word out of their hearts, lest they should believe and be saved. But the ones on the rock are those who, when they hear, receive the word with joy; and these have no root, who believe for a while and in time of temptation fall away. And the ones that fell among thorns are those who, when they have heard, go out and are chocked with cares, riches, and pleasures of life, and bring no fruit to maturity. But the ones that fell on the good ground are those who, having heard the word with a noble and good heart, keep it and bear fruit with patience." Luke 8: 10-15.

Beware, brethren, lest there be in any of you an evil heart of unbelief in departing from the living God; but exhort one another daily, while it is called "today" lest any of you be hardened through the deceitfulness of sin. For we have become partakers of Christ if we hold the beginning of our confidence steadfast to the end, while it is said, 'Today, if you will hear His voice, do not harden your hearts as in the rebellion.' (Hebrew 3:12–15)

Jesus loves us so much that He wants us to spend eternity with Him. Before He went to heaven, He said to the believers, "Let not your heart be troubled; you believe in God, believe also in Me. In my father's house are many mansions; if it were not so, I would have told you. I go to prepare a place for you. And if I go and prepare a place for you, I will come again and receive you to Myself; that where I am, there you may be also. And where I go you know, and the way you know"(John 14:1–4).

God does not want anyone to perish; He wants all people to come to repentance so they can be with Him forever and ever and ever. As the apostle Peter wrote, "The Lord is not slack concerning His promise, as some count slackness, but is longsuffering towards us, not willing that any should perish but that all should come to repentance" (2 Peter 3:9).

Emphasizing that man should spend eternity with Him, Jesus said, "And if your right eye causes you to sin, pluck it out and cast it from you; for it is more profitable for you that one of your members perish, than for your whole body to be cast into hell. And if your right hand causes you to sin, cut it off and cast it from you; for it is more profitable for you that one of your members perish, than for your whole body to be cast into hell" (Matthew 5:29–30). Jesus is saying here that whatever we need to do to get in there, we should do. He is saying that we need to get into heaven, no matter the cost.

Jesus wants His followers to shine in the world:

> "You are the salt of the earth; but if the salt loses its flavor, how shall it become seasoned? It is then good for nothing but to be thrown out and trampled underfoot by men. You are the light of the world. A city that is set on a hill cannot be hidden. Nor do they light a lamp and put it under a basket, but on a lamp stand, and it gives light to all who are in the house. Let your light so shine before men, that they may see your good works and glorify your Father in heaven." (Matthew 5:13–16)

Jesus commands those who are called Christians to be the "salt and light" of the world. A Christian's conversation should be seasoned with God's wisdom, which comes only from His Word. Our conversation should be soothing and comforting to someone who is hurting, discouraged, downhearted, or dismayed. It should be a balm to someone going through tribulation, sickness, or hopelessness.

A Christian is called to be "light of the world." Where do we get this light? Just as the moon gets its light from the sun, so Christians get their light from Jesus, because He said, "I am the light of the world." How do Christians get this light from Christ? By being connected to Him and by abiding in Him. The Spirit that lives within us will guide, direct, and enable us to do so.

The world is watching and expecting Christians to exhibit Jesus' virtues through their lives. Followers of Jesus Christ have an awesome yet pleasant duty and responsibility to follow and practice His teachings. They are required to exhibit His virtues for their own benefit and for the good of the world.

Chapter 9

Conclusion

More than 360 prophecies about Jesus' birth, life, and mission were recorded in the Bible hundreds of years before He was born in Bethlehem. Most of these prophecies have been fulfilled with a pinpoint accuracy, while others are being fulfilled. Isaiah was one of the prophets through whom God spoke about Jesus' birth, His life and mission. Here's what the prophet Isaiah prophesied more than seven hundred years before the birth of Christ:

> Who has believed our report? And to whom has the arm of the Lord been revealed? For He shall grow up before Him as a tender plant, and as a root out of dry ground. He has no form or comeliness; and when we see Him, there is no beauty that we should desire Him. He is despised and rejected by men, a Man of sorrows and acquainted with grief. And we hid, as it were, our faces from Him; He was despised, and we did not esteem Him. Surely He has borne our griefs and carried our sorrows; yet we esteemed Him stricken, smitten by God, and afflicted. But He was wounded for our transgressions, He was bruised for our

iniquities; the chastisement for our peace was upon Him, and by His stripes we are healed. All we like sheep have gone astray; we have turned, everyone, to his own way; and the Lord has laid on Him the iniquity of us all. He was oppressed and He was afflicted, yet He opened not His mouth; He was led as a lamb to the slaughter, and as a sheep before its shearers is silent, so He opened not His mouth. He was taken from prison and from judgment, and who will declare His generation? For He was cut off from the land of the living; for the transgressions of my people He was stricken. And they made His grave with the wicked—but with the rich at His death, because He had done no violence, Nor was any deceit in His mouth. Yet it pleased the Lord to bruise Him; He has put Him to grief. When You make His soul an offering for sin, He shall see His seed, He shall prolong His days, and the pleasure of the Lord shall prosper in His hand. He shall see the travail of His soul, and be satisfied. By His knowledge My righteous Servant shall justify many, for He shall bear their iniquities. Therefore I will divide Him a portion with the great, and He shall divide the spoil with the strong, because He poured out His soul unto death, and He was numbered with the transgressors, and He bore the sin of many, and made intercession for the transgressors. (Isaiah 53:1–12)

Many biblical scholars consider this prophecy one of the most important texts in the Bible. It briefly describes the birth, life, crucifixion, and death of Jesus Christ. People from different walks of life have expressed and confessed that their lives have been transformed because of reading and studying Isaiah's prophecy about Jesus Christ. This surely has affected my life in a positive way.

Although each verse of this chapter is loaded and needs much elaboration, I will touch briefly on the main points. I encourage you to dig further into Isaiah 53 and glean the rich treasure God has revealed through His prophet.

This amazing message brings good tidings for all time and eternity. Who would have believed the humiliation and suffering the Messiah would undergo because of His selfless love and sacrifice for humankind? He is referred to as the arm of the Lord because the power of the Almighty God rested on Him. The Messiah, or Jesus Christ, would grow before God with complete submissiveness.

Jesus was born at a time when spiritual darkness and sin was all around. The dry ground here refers to a barren and lifeless nation going through religious motions and rituals but bearing no fruit that would lead to positive spiritual effects. People, including the religious leaders were religious, but lost. The rulers of that day oppressed them, and they were looking for a Messiah who would deliver them from their woes. But when Jesus was born, very few recognized Him, because He was born into a very ordinary working-class family and led a very humble life. Nothing about His appearance drew people to Him. The religious leaders of that day did not like Him, because He chided them openly. They found His character unappealing. Those who were drawn to Him were drawn because of the beauty of His righteous life, His teachings, and His miracles.

Christ's teaching was contrary to the teaching of His day. He knew He would be hated, reviled, and rejected. Because of sin, we deserve suffering, pain, and punishment, but He took all of it upon Himself. The chastisement that Jesus suffered for our sake brought us peace with God, thereby saving us from our sins.

Silently He submitted Himself for our sins. He willingly gave Himself to the rulers and religious leaders of that day. He put up no resistance; He did not protest or complain in self-defense. He did everything willingly so that we who were doomed sinners might be saved. He was delivered from oppression and punishment only by horrible death. He was not given a fair hearing. No one would stand by His side when He was presented before the authorities to be judged and punished. Everyone abandoned Him. No one defended Him. He bore it all alone.

The rulers and religious leaders of that day crucified Jesus between two thieves in an effort to prove He was a criminal, despite the fact that they could not prove Him guilty. Having given up His life for transgressors, He was placed with them in death. He suffered the fate of a sinner though there was no sin in His life, nor did He commit any crime. He was buried in the tomb of a rich man.

It did not please God that His Servant, the Messiah, should suffer. But to deliver humanity from the bondage of sin and for the plan of salvation to succeed, it was the only way.

"It pleased the Lord" means it was the Lord's will that His Servant, Jesus, should suffer for our sins. Christ's suffering was part of the eternal plan of salvation. The human race had lost its innocence, its capacity to love and obey God, its dominion over the earth, and even its life. Christ came to restore all these permanently by giving up His life. This sacrifice was essential to our redemption and restoration. And when He comes again, multitudes will believe in Him

Jesus endured the cross in view of the joy that was set before Him—the joy over sinners being saved and reconciled to God. Keeping this very important task in view, Jesus took delight in performing the will of His Father. He laid down His life to win eternal salvation for humankind.

Christ would see the result of the travail or the labor of His soul. His sacrifice would not be in vain. Because of His death, many would live. And because of His sufferings, many would find peace, healing, and joy.

God will reward His triumphant servant with a place of high honor. All that had been lost as a result of sin will be restored. Christ has rescued humankind from the hand of the enemy. And we share in His triumph, not as slaves or servants, but as people redeemed by His blood and destined to reign with Him forever. Therefore, Jesus will receive a name above every name, one before which every knee will bow.

What an honor and a privilege for those who put their faith in Christ that they will not only share His triumph over the enemy and death, but also reign with Him forever and ever.

Because humanity has committed high treason by disobeying God's command, all humans have earned the penalty, which is death: "For the wages of sin is death" (Romans 6:23). If I defy a physical or scientific law, I have to face the consequences. If I touch a live electric wire, I will be electrocuted. If I throw myself from a high cliff, I'll die. Similarly, if I break God's divine law, a penalty has to be paid, and that penalty is death. All have sinned, and the death penalty hangs over everyone.

God knew that a savior needed to die for the sins of the world: "[Know] that you were not redeemed with corruptible things, like silver or gold, from your aimless conduct received by tradition from your father, but with the precious blood of Christ as of a lamb without blemish and without spot. He indeed was foreordained before the foundation of the world, but was manifest in these last times for you who through Him believe in God, who raised Him from the dead and gave Him glory, so that your faith and hope are in God" (1 Peter 1:18–21).

The cleansing of sin and reconciliation to God is by the shed blood of Jesus Christ, our Savior. Without His sacrifice, our sins cannot be washed away. Jesus Christ paid the penalty for our sins, making forgiveness possible. "And He Himself is the propitiation for our sins, and not for ours only but also for the whole world" (1 John 2:2). No human teaching or knowledge can cause our sins to be forgiven. Only Christ's sacrifice can permanently cleanse and forgive our sins.

Chapter 10

An Invitation

God has in place the plan of salvation. He has created a way through His Son Jesus Christ, so humankind may be saved from eternal damnation. He has offered us the free gift of salvation. We do not have to work for it or earn it. It is absolutely free. It is there for the asking.

It is up to us to accept His invitation or reject it. God has endowed us with a free will. We can make our own choices. We are free to love God and accept His free gift of salvation if we want to. God has laid down His precepts so we can tread the right path. But He does not force anyone to obey Him or do His will. "I call heaven and earth as witnesses today against you, that I have set before you life and death, blessing and cursing; therefore choose life, that both you and your descendants may live" (Deuteronomy 30:19).

He speaks to us through His Spirit in a "still small voice." It is up to us to heed God's voice and obey Him, or choose our own ways and do whatever we want to do and follow whatever path we want to.

God loves us so much that He wants us to be with Him forever. Therefore He extends His salvation plan and invites everyone to receive it. But it is up to each individual to accept it. Jesus wants to live in the human heart, so He can have fellowship with him. He says, "Behold, I stand at the door and knock. If anyone hears My voice and opens the door, I will come in to him and dine with him, and he with Me" (Revelation 3:20). The invitation is free and is for anyone and everyone who accepts it. There are no conditions other than opening the doors of our hearts and receiving Him.

The whole plan of salvation is in place. All we have to do is accept it, and we will be one with the Lord once again. "On the last day, that great day of the feast, Jesus stood and cried out, saying, if anyone thirsts, let him come to Me and drink. He who believes in Me, as the Scripture has said, out of his heart will flow rivers of living water [the Holy Spirit]" (John 7:37–38).

The work of redemption is complete, and God has extended the invitation to everyone. Here's an illustration Jesus gave:

> "A certain man gave a great supper and invited many, and sent his servant at supper time to say to those who were invited, come for all things are now ready. But they all with one accord began to make excuses. The first said to him, 'I have bought a piece of ground, and I must go and see it. I ask you to have me excused.' And another said, 'I have bought five yoke of oxen and I am going to test them. I ask you to have me excused.' Still another said, 'I have married a wife, and therefore I cannot come.' So that servant came and reported these things to his master. Then the master of the house, being angry, said to his servant, 'Go out quickly into the streets and lanes of the city, and bring in here the poor and the maimed and the lame and the blind.' And the servant said, 'Master, it is done as you commanded, and still there is room.' Then the master said to the servant, 'Go out into the

highways and hedges, and compel them to come in, that my house may be filled. For I say to you that none of those men who were invited shall taste my supper.'" (Luke 14:15-24)

In this illustration, a man prepared a feast and invited his friends to come, eat, and have fellowship with him, but they all found excuses. The excuses they all gave were poor ones. They really didn't care about the invitation, which enraged the man. He told his servant to invite the poor, the maimed, the lame, and the blind, so they can partake of the supper he had prepared.

Talking about Jesus, John the evangelist wrote, "He came to His own, and His own did not receive Him. But as many as received Him, to them He gave the right to become children of God, to those who believed in His name: who were born, not of blood, nor of the will of the flesh, nor of the will of man, but of God" (John 1:11–13).

The Days of Noah

We are seeing drastic changes in weather patterns, politics, morality, human behavior, and so on. Humankind is very busy buying and selling, sowing, reaping, accumulating wealth, marrying and giving in marriage—and has very little or no time for God. From time to time, God has given enough warning to humankind through His prophets, and Jesus Himself gave warnings beforehand, so humans would repent and be saved. The same conditions prevailed at Noah's time—people were engaged in business, sowing, reaping, getting married and giving in marriage—until the flood came and they perished, except for Noah's family. And, as Peter wrote, "Scoffers will come in the last days, walking according to their own lusts, and saying, where is the promise of His coming? For since the fathers fell asleep, all things continue as they were from the beginning of creation" (2 Peter 3:3–4). Even today, people are mocking and saying, "When is Christ coming again?" Friends, His coming is imminent. All the signs are pointing to it.

But are we ready to receive Him? God is longsuffering. He does not want anyone to perish; He wants all to repent. Jesus warned,

> "As it was in the days of Noah, so it will be also in the days of the Son of Man: They ate, they drank, they married wives, they were given in marriage, until the day that Noah entered the ark, and the flood came and destroyed them all. Likewise as it was also in the days of Lot: They ate, they drank, they bought, they sold, they planted, they built; but on the day that Lot went out of Sodom it rained fire and brimstone from heaven and destroyed them all. Even so will it be in the day when the Son of Man is revealed." (Luke 17:26–30).

Let's take a look around us: people are busy buying, selling, marrying, planting, and harvesting, just like people were doing at the time of Noah. They did not heed God's warning, but mocked. The floods came, and they were all destroyed.

> "But Noah found grace in the eyes of the Lord. This is the genealogy of Noah. Noah was a just man, perfect in his generations. Noah walked with God. And Noah begot three sons: Shem, Ham and Japheth. The earth also was corrupt before God, and the earth was filled with violence. So God looked upon the earth and in deed it was corrupt; for all flesh had corrupted their way on the earth. And God said to Noah, "The end of all flesh has come before Me, for the earth is filled with violence through them, and behold, I will destroy them with the earth." (Genesis 6:8–13)

Today we live in a world constantly threatened by wars, rumors of wars, unrest, troubled people, and violence. In the cities, there are hate crimes, drive-by shootings, mothers killing their own children. There is lawlessness and no real accountability. We are becoming more tolerant and less moral. And it is not going to get any better. If anything, it is getting worse. What is humanity to do? Amid all this confusion and chaos, we are to turn to God and ask Him to guide and direct us so we are drawn closer to Him and are spared from His wrath.

Now the Good News

By giving His life for sinners, Jesus has opened the door of heaven, which was shut because of sin. He defeated Satan at the cross, and by His resurrection, He crushed Satan's head forever. Satan trembles at the name of Jesus, and he flees at the mention of it. There is power in the name of Jesus and healing in His blood. Also, His blood cleanses all unrighteousness and sin.

By accepting Jesus as your Lord and Savior, you inherit numerous promises and rights in Him, such as:

- You are God's child (John 1:12).
- You are a citizen of heaven (Philippians 3:20).
- You are victorious (1 Corinthians 15:57).
- You are born again (1 Peter 1:23).
- You are set free (Romans 8:2; John 8:32).
- You can approach God with freedom and confidence (Ephesians 3:12).
- You are free from the law of sin and death (Romans 8:2).
- You have the peace of God that passes all understanding (Philippians 4:7).

- Greater is He Who (Jesus) is in you than he (Satan) who is in the world (1 John 4:4).
- You are God's child, for you are born again of the incorruptible seed of the Word of God, which lives and abides forever (1 Peter 1:23).
- You are the temple of the Holy Spirit; You are not your own (1 Corinthians 6:19).
- You are the light of the world (Matthew 5:14).
- You are forgiven of all your sins and washed in the blood of Jesus (Ephesians 1:7).
- You are delivered from the power of darkness and translated into God's kingdom (Colossians 1:13).
- You are redeemed from the curse of sin, sickness, and poverty (Galatians 3:13).
- You are called of God to be the voice of His praise (2 Timothy 1:9).
- You are healed by the stripes of Jesus (Isaiah 53:5; 1 Peter 2:24.)
- The devil flees from you because you resist him in the name of Jesus (James 4:7).
- God has not given you a spirit of fear; but of power, love, and a sound mind (2 Timothy 1:7).
- It is not you who live, but Christ lives in you (Galatians 2:20).

These are a few of God's promises; there is a host of other promises and rights mentioned in the Word of God that a child of God inherits when he or she repents from sin and accepts Jesus as Lord and Savior.

Saved by His Grace

On the judgment day, God will ask me why He should let me into His heaven, to which my answer would be, "Because your Son Jesus Christ died for my sins."

The blood of Christ has cleansed me of my sins and has granted me the right and privilege to live with Him in heaven forever. Only by His grace can I enter into heaven—and not because of my good works or on my own merits. I cannot earn my salvation. None of us is capable of doing that. It is a free gift of God for everyone who believes on His Son.

It takes only one sin to negate all my good works, no matter how many good deeds I have. Suppose I am making an omelet with five eggs. I crack four eggs and throw them in the frying pan, and they're all good. After cracking the fifth and throwing in the pan, I find out it's rotten. No one will eat this omelet, because this last egg has spoiled the four good eggs. In the same way, I can do all the good I want, but my one bad action spoils all my good works.

Jesus Is the King, the Prophet, the Priest, and More

We have seen that Jesus has many titles. He is the Son of God. He is the King of kings, and He is unparalleled. There is no one like Him. He is "Wonderful, Counselor, Mighty God, Everlasting Father, Prince of Peace" (Isaiah 9:6). I accept Jesus in His complete form and with all the titles that go with His name. If I accept Him only as a teacher or only as a prophet or only as a good person or as one of the gods, I am not accepting the Jesus Christ who came to this earth two thousand years ago in the human form to save humankind from his sin and eternal damnation. If I accept only a part of Him, I deny His completeness.

Do you accept Jesus Christ, the Son of God, and believe He is your personal Lord and Savior? If you have not done this before, I would encourage you to take the action now and accept Him as the Lord of your life. He is waiting for you with outstretched arms and will surely accept you as His child. This is His promise, and He is ever true to His promises. The Word of God says, "That if you confess with your mouth the Lord Jesus and believe in your heart that God has raised Him from the dead, you will be saved. For with the heart one believes to righteousness, and with the mouth confession is made to salvation. For the Scripture says, whoever believes on Him will not be put to shame" (Romans 10:9–11).

Jesus said, "All that the Father gives Me will come to Me, and the one who comes to Me I will by no means cast out," (John 6:37).

If after reading this book and knowing about Jesus, you have come to the conclusion that you would like to give your life to Christ, here is a simple and short prayer you can recite:

Salvation Prayer

Dear God, I come to you in the name of Jesus. I acknowledge that I am a sinner and am sorry for my sins and ask for Your forgiveness. I believe that Jesus Christ died on the cross for my sins, and I now turn from my sins. I accept Jesus as my Lord and Savior. Thank you, Jesus, for dying for me and giving me eternal life. Amen

If you've said this prayer you are "born again," which means you are born for the second time. The first time you were born physically into this world, but now you are born spiritually.

God never forces anyone to accept Jesus as Savior. He simply extends an invitation to all who want to have their sins forgiven and want to spend eternity with Him in heaven. Salvation is a free gift, paid for by the precious blood of Jesus, "knowing that you were not redeemed with corruptible things, like silver or gold, from your aimless conduct received by tradition from your fathers but with the precious blood of Christ, as of a lamb without blemish and without spot" (1 Peter 1:18–19). By confessing our sins and accepting Jesus as Lord and Savior, we accept this free gift of salvation.

When a person is born again, God the Father and God the Son come into his or her heart in the form of the Holy Spirit. Jesus said, "If anyone loves Me, he will keep My word; and My Father will love him, and We will come to him and make Our home with him" (John 14:23). Having the the Holy Spirit in you truly means God is within you. You have God living in your body: "But you are not in the flesh but in the Spirit, if indeed the Spirit of God dwells in you. Now if anyone does not have the Spirit of Christ, he is not His" (Romans 8:9). This means that the Spirit of Christ dwells within every believer.

The Holy Spirit guides all born-again people, comforts them, teaches them, rebukes them, chastises them, convicts them, encourages them, empowers them, loves them, strengthens them, and more. The Holy Spirit molds believers according to the Word of God. We need to be very sensitive to the Holy Spirit and heed His "still small voice." We have to be attuned to Him. One way to do this is to regularly read the Word of God. In this process, God will never leave us nor forsake us: "Let your conduct be without covetousness, and be content with such things as you have. For He Himself has said, I will never leave you nor forsake you" (Hebrew 13:5).

By accepting Jesus Christ as our Lord and Savior, we become new creations: "Therefore, if anyone is in Christ, he is a new creation; old things have passed away; behold, all things have become new" (2 Corinthians 5:17).

Now that you are born again, you need to find a Bible-based, Bible-teaching church, study God's Word, and be baptized.

May God bless you abundantly and may the Holy Spirit guide you.

Let's Be Ready for the Ultimate Judgment of God

Then I saw a great white throne and Him who sat on it, from whose face the earth and the heaven fled away. And there was found no place for them. And I saw the dead, small and great, standing before God, and books were opened. And another book was opened, which is the Book of Life. And the dead were judged according to their works, by the things which were written in the books. The sea gave up the dead who were in it, and death and Hades delivered up the dead who were in them. And they were judged, each one according to his works. Then death and Hades were cast into the lake of fire. This is the second death. And anyone not found written in the book of life was cast into the lake of fire. (Revelation 20:11–15)

"And behold, I am coming quickly, and My reward is with Me, to give to every one according to his work. I am the Alpha and the Omega, the Beginning and the End, the First and the Last. Blessed are those who do His commandments, that they may have the right to the tree of life and may enter through the gates into the city. But outside are dogs and sorcerers and sexually immoral and murderers and idolaters, and whoever loves and practices a lie. I, Jesus, have sent My angel to testify to you these things in the churches. I am the Root and the Offspring of David, the Bright and Morning Star. And the Spirit and the bride say, come and let him who hears say come! And let him to thirsts come. And whoever desires, let him take the water of life freely." (Revelation 22:12–17)

Amen and amen. Come, Lord Jesus!

Afterword

I have attempted to briefly introduce or reintroduce Jesus to the reader. If this has touched you, I advise you to dig further into the Word of God and become His disciple, if you have not done this already. If you decide not to, I thank you for your time. May the Lord richly bless you and yours.

About the Author

John has lived with his wife, Marilyn, in Edmonton, Alberta, since 1972. Together they have three children, Sarah, Sabrina, and Sean, and two grandchildren, Anisha and Rashaun.

Having been born into a Christian family, John was raised in church and in a Christian atmosphere. He started learning the Bible at a very early age. He knew many Bible verses and won several prizes in Bible competitions. During his childhood and youth, he was considered to be a good person. But that was not enough. He knew he had to repent from his sins and accept Jesus as his Lord and Savior, but he said to himself that he still has a lot of time to do that.

After John finished high school, he decided to get serious about getting closer to God. He was searching for peace within. He studied the Word of God and prayed, repented of his sins, and gave his life to Jesus Christ. He was subsequently baptized and now has the assurance that Jesus lives in his heart. The Word of God, the Holy Bible gives us this assurance: "The Spirit Himself bears witness with our spirit that we are children of God, and if children, the heirs—heirs of God and joint heirs with Christ, if indeed we suffer with Him, that we may also be glorified together" (Romans 8:16–17).

When John accepted Jesus as his Lord and Savior, he inherited a lot of His promises and blessings. He has attempted to write this book in an effort to introduce many to Jesus, sharing those promises and blessing with them.

May God bless you richly.

CPSIA information can be obtained at www.ICGtesting.com
Printed in the USA
LVOW082334010113

313953LV00001B/4/P